Zonas Peligrosas

POLIS: Fordham Series in Urban Studies

Edited by Daniel J. Monti, Saint Louis University

POLIS will address the questions of what makes a good community and how urban dwellers succeed and fail to live up to the idea that people from various backgrounds and levels of society can live together effectively, if not always congenially. The series is the province of no single discipline; we are searching for authors in fields as diverse as American studies, anthropology, history, political science, sociology, and urban studies who can write for both academic and informed lay audiences. Our objective is to celebrate and critically assess the customary ways in which urbanites make the world corrigible for themselves and the other kinds of people with whom they come into contact every day.

To this end, we will publish both book-length manuscripts and a series of "digital shorts" (e-books) focusing on case studies of groups, locales, and events that provide clues as to how urban people accomplish this delicate and exciting task. We expect to publish one or two books every year but a larger number of "digital shorts." The digital shorts will be 20,000 words or fewer and have a strong narrative voice.

Series Advisory Board:

Zonas Peligrosas

THE CHALLENGE OF CREATING SAFE
NEIGHBORHOODS IN CENTRAL AMERICA

Tom Hare

FORDHAM UNIVERSITY PRESS
New York   2018

Fordham University Press has no responsibility for
the persistence or accuracy of URLs for external
or third-party Internet websites referred to in this
publication and does not guarantee that any content on such websites is, or will remain, accurate
or appropriate.

Fordham University Press also publishes its books
in a variety of electronic formats. Some content
that appears in print may not be available in
electronic books.

Visit us online at www.fordhampress.com.

Library of Congress Control Number: 2018933433

Printed in the United States of America

20 19 18   5 4 3 2 1

First edition

for my family
and for all those who work tirelessly to create safe
neighborhoods

CONTENTS

Preface

El Paseo is the new "place to be" in Greater San Salvador. In a city with few public spaces, it is unrivaled in its fusion of colonial charm, courtyard cafés, and kitschy shops. The new sidewalks, working streetlights, and brightly painted buildings stretch for several blocks along a pedestrians-only street. The novelty of the area draws an eclectic mix of young and old, rich and poor. This is unusual in a city that is divided by high walls and barbed wire into exclusive enclaves versus marginal communities, and "*zonas seguras*" versus "*zonas peligrosas*." It is even more unusual given that many strangers have learned to fear one another because of the high rates of crime and victimization that make San Salvador one of the most violent cities in the world. Along *El Paseo*, however, families push their kids in strollers, elderly couples cruise on rented tandem bikes, and working-class couples sit elbow to elbow with wealthy couples, both out for a glass of wine.

Walking along *El Paseo* one night, I was swept up in the energy and excitement of the crowds. A band played rock music in an empty lot-*cum*-public stage. Crowds gathered around to hear the music, stopping momentarily on their way to dinner, to meet friends for a drink, or just to walk in one of the only secure parts

Figure 1. El Paseo at night. (Source: El Salvador Travel Network.)

of the city. Food vendors lined the sidewalk with their carts and the street with tables, adding to the carnivalesque feel. The restaurants and storefronts were the shoreline for a river of people mixing and mingling. A man, one of the many Salvadorans who have migrated to the United States and who come back infrequently, struck up a conversation with me. Crazy, he said; I am from this neighborhood and it was nothing like this when I left.

Indeed, it was nothing like this before the mayor of Santa Tecla decided it was time to revive this deteriorating suburb of San Salvador. In the early 2000s, crime and violence, endemically high, were on the rise again. Migrants, such as the man I met, were leaving town and the country for opportunities in other, more secure places. There was not a lot of money to work with, but international donors and local businesses were supportive. The mayor called together a group of officials, citizens, and businesspeople to create a plan for the city. He wanted change, but he wanted the participation of as many people as possible on a citizen's council to determine the best course of action. The council, together with elected officials, determined that *Paseo el Carmen* (*El Paseo*'s official name) should be created and the nearby park rehabilitated, social programs should engage more youth, and the municipal preventative police force should be reformed and made more effective with better crime data.

The plan was set into motion. Only a few short years later, the homicide rate had been cut by two-thirds in the city (*Alcaldía Municipal de Santa Tecla*, 2012). Other crimes against persons and property were down. Santa Tecla had made a name for itself, not only as a family and nightlife destination among Salvadorans but also as a showcase for crime prevention for international donors. Here was a town that had come together with the direct participation of citizens to effectively reduce crime as rates continued to soar around the country.

Compared with other nights walking along similar streets in the area, I did feel safe the night I walked along *El Paseo*. There were a few dark corners here and there, but the large number of people enjoying themselves increased my sense of security. People were civil to one another, kept the street free of trash, and were generally unconcerned with much else other than enjoying the evening. It seemed that the space had indeed transformed the community and social life of those who inhabited or, at least, passed through it. The street created an inviting, organized space where people, no matter their class or background, could come together. *El Paseo* seemed to promote social order through better physical order. By all accounts, it appeared to be the urban redevelopment success story that friends, colleagues, and international aid agencies touted it to be.

Then came the soldiers. Walking single-file briskly through the throngs of people, they were clad in their olive green uniforms and carried large automatic weapons. The crowds parted in front of them, but no one seemed really to take notice of their presence. In fact, soldiers such as these are a staple of many streetscapes across San Salvador. For more than a decade now they have been out of their barracks as a central part of "*mano dura*" or "heavy-handed" crime-reduction efforts. The soldiers are a literal manifestation of the "war on crime" throughout El Salvador.

The soldiers were a reminder that there was a lot more going on to prevent crime and provide a sense of security than just a pretty street where people come together. Apparently, even a nice-looking place full of people who seemed to get along just fine needed reinforcements to deter criminals. The mayor's efforts at beautification and social organization seemed to have something to do with crime prevention, but surely so too did the heavily armed soldiers. I was witnessing firsthand the tension between the two preferred approaches to public security in El Salvador and across Central America: one based on crime prevention through social organization, and the other based on crime repression through militarized policing.

As I witnessed that night, the two approaches are certainly not mutually exclusive. Nevertheless, the country is divided as to which approach—prevention or repression—should take precedence in policy making and planning. The 2014 presidential election was evidence of this divide. It was in large part a referendum on security policy, given that the biggest concern cited by voters was insecurity. At 59 percent, it was the most concerned voters had ever been about security, and it was far ahead of other concerns, such as jobs and the economy (Segura, 2014). The presidential and vice-presidential candidates on the right campaigned to strengthen the "war on crime" approach. The candidates on the left, which included the then-mayor of Santa Tecla as the vice-presidential candidate, campaigned on the crime-prevention approach. They pointed to the success of interventions such as *El Paseo* and the town's social programs. Even after a second round of voting, the race was essentially a tie. Half of the Salvadoran populace favored the repressive approach, and half favored the preventative approach. In the end, a margin of just 6,000 votes (0.22 percent) favored the candidates on the left (Meléndez, 2014). Since the election, however, the administration has largely continued existing policies with more repression than prevention. Campaign promises to replicate urban renewal projects like *El Paseo* in other parts of the city and country have not been fulfilled. San Salvador remains one of the most violent cities in the world.

Zonas Peligrosas

CHAPTER 1

Citizen Security

After hearing about the problems of neighborhood crime and violence in San Salvador for many years, experiencing a sense of insecurity firsthand, grieving with friends victimized by violence, and then witnessing prevention efforts like *El Paseo*, I became more interested in the community life of Salvadoran neighborhoods. I started to ask myself: How do residents use public spaces? How do they come together in places without secure spaces? How do they participate in decisionmaking processes? Are there differences in community and social life between communities with different physical appearances? And, what does this all have to do with whether or not a neighborhood is a *"zona segura"* or *"zona peligrosa"*? I wanted to know if community and social life is really any different in neighborhoods with and without attempted "fixes" to the social or physical order.

I also wanted to know more about the theories and hypotheses about life in these neighborhoods that undergird the popular concept of "citizen security." Citizen security is a prevalent policy approach to crime and violence prevention in Central America that emphasizes physical order, strong social cohesion, participation, and expectations for action on the part of neighbors and civil

1

society. I quickly learned that the idea behind the *El Paseo* citizen security approach is nothing new. Fixing up rundown areas to make people feel and act better was an approach attempted by urban social reformers in nineteenth-century Europe. It became established by the mid-twentieth century in the United States. Many of the prescriptions offered in the literature on citizen security in Central America draw on "social disorganization theory" or the "disorganization hypothesis" from the United States. Basically, theorists who ascribe to this hypothesis see two sides to the disorganization of a neighborhood. One is social, where there is little engagement by neighbors, a lack of community life, and problems maintaining order that is evinced by crime and violence. The other is physical, where one can observe deteriorated buildings, disrepair in streets and sidewalks, and a lot of people crowded into small areas. Both the social and physical sides are assumed to be related in the hypothesis. Where there is physical disorder, we should expect to find social disorder. When the physical disorder is fixed, one should expect to see improvements on the social side, including a reduction in crime.

From the outside, this seemed to be the case in Santa Tecla. Physical order was created, improving the social order such that a crowd could gather to enjoy a night out in the middle of one of the most violent cities in the world. Similar to what I witnessed, proponents of the disorganization hypothesis suggested that physical things such as deterioration and population density correspond to social things such as a lack of strong social ties and high levels of crime (Greenberg, Rohe, & Williams, 1982; Jacobs, 1961; Kelling & Wilson, 1982; Newman, 1972; Park, 1915; Park & Burgess, 1925; Shaw & McKay, 1942). European social reformers leaned on this hypothesis as a way to fix early urban problems of poverty and crime. They assumed that the rise in crime in late-nineteenth-century cities was attributable to rapid, disorderly urbanization.

This hypothesis was criticized at the time by European social ecologists André-Michel Guerry (1833) and R. W. Rawson (1839). Guerry and Rawson were among the first to determine that there was significant variation in crime even within urban areas. They found that, contrary to anti-urban narratives, it was not the trend in industrialization and the unpleasant aesthetics of early urbanization that increased crime, but spatially differentiated social order within those urban areas. Tight, shared spaces and the way streets were organized mattered less than what people did in those spaces. For instance, Guerry found that crime was concentrated in industrial areas in France, while Rawson found that non-industrial areas in England had the most crime. It was not the ugly and dirty urban industrial area itself that invited crime, as people had thought previously. There was something different going on.

In the United States, however, the idea that living closer together in an urban area increased crime and violence was accepted well into the twentieth century. The concentration of unemployment, family disintegration, poverty, and crime was believed to make these problems worse than in rural areas (Hall, 2002). After the turn of the century, it was the Chicago School sociologists who looked at these issues most closely. They advanced what would become "social disorganization theory" in urban areas. While European predecessors and Chicago contemporaries set the stage, Clifford Shaw and Henry McKay (1942) are credited with the theory that crime is perpetuated depending on the amount of disorganization of a particular neighborhood. The definition of social disorganization used by Shaw and McKay is summarized well by Sampson (2012) as "The inability of a community to realize the common values of its residents and maintain effective social controls" (p. 37). This inability to realize common values in disorganized communities was a result of some of the same "urban problems" identified by earlier theorists. In particular, Shaw and McKay pointed to heterogeneous populations, migration, and weak interpersonal relationships as the source of disorganization. Greater varieties of people and more of them meant that they would not share the same idea of what was important. Without a basic, if implicit, agreement among these peoples about the maintenance of private property and public spaces, how to interact or work together, there could be no effective way to maintain order.

Social and physical reform programs in the United States picked up on these ideas in an effort to combat rising crime and violence in cities. For example, the Chicago Area Projects, started by Shaw in the 1930s, instituted community committees and promoted youth participation in decision making. The Mobilization for Youth program in New York, begun in the 1960s, promoted physical and social order through neighborhood councils, the beautification of public spaces, and greater public participation in policy discussions.

While evaluation methodology was poor during the early days of the Chicago Area Projects, by the time of Mobilization for Youth evaluations were calling into question programs that relied primarily on social cohesion and participation (Klein, 1995, p. 141). After decades of proliferation, regard for the disorganization hypothesis began to recede toward the end of the twentieth century in the United States. It drew fire from both researchers and practitioners as the epidemic of crime and violence continued to spread across the country after a half-century of prevention efforts tried to fix physically and socially disordered neighborhoods (Klein, 1995; Lees, 1991; Monti, 1994; Spergel, 1995).

Alternative approaches based on a retooled version of the disorganization hypothesis, such as "collective efficacy," emerged to refine disorganization theory (Sampson, Raudenbush, & Earls, 1997; Sampson, 2004). Explanations based on the idea of collective efficacy placed greater emphasis on the perception of social control than the observed amount of physical order in a neighborhood. Collective efficacy has been shown to better predict amounts of crime and violence than indicators of disorganization theory in some neighborhoods in the United States (Sampson, 2012).

At the same time the disorganization hypothesis was being criticized, citizen security prescriptions were being developed to combat increasing crime and violence in Latin America (Bergman, 2006). Along with reforms to police, prosecutors, and the courts, fixing the physical appearance of a neighborhood and strengthening the participation and cohesion of the community within it became prevalent citizen security interventions in Latin America (Tulchin & Golding, 2003). These were fixes that included infrastructure investment and social programs, all with a participatory bent (Chinchilla, 2003; UNDP, 2009a; UNDP, 2009b; UNDP, 2009c; UNDP, 2013; UNODC, 2007; USAID, 2010; World Bank, 2011). This mirrors what social reformers had tried for more than a century in Europe and the United States, and what I witnessed along *El Paseo*.

Despite a large amount of prescriptive literature describing what neighborhoods and communities should do, and descriptive literature telling what neighborhoods and communities actually do, empirical evaluations showing the impact of the citizen security approach are nascent and show mixed results (Abt & Wiship, 2016; Bergman, 2006; Frühling, 2012). For example, evaluations using representative samples in the greater Santiago, Chile, metropolitan area demonstrated that social disadvantage (e.g., poverty) and physical disorder and deterioration are associated with greater incidence of crime, while trust is associated with lesser incidence of crime (Frühling & Gallardo, 2012; Olavarría-Gambi & Allende-González, 2014). Findings from Brazil show that while poverty and physical disorder are associated with each other, neither is associated with crime (Villareal & Silva, 2006). However, social disadvantage and homicide are associated in the same areas (Silva, 2014). In Colombia, social disadvantage and homicide are associated, but environmental or physical factors are much less associated (Escobar, 2012). Finally, in Mexico, collective efficacy and social cohesion correlate well with a sense of security (Valenzuela Aguilera, 2012). These mixed and nuanced findings, along with success stories such as *El Paseo*, are promising (Washington Office on Latin America & Inter-American Development Bank , 2011). However, they must be considered along with the challenge of generalizability across cultural and crime contexts within the region and between the region and more-developed countries (Timerman, 2013; Tulchin & Golding, 2003). In particular, the fact that social disadvantage often increases cohesion in the region confounds the original disorganization hypothesis. Poor Latin Americans, it has been found, are more likely to band together to provide for basic needs than others, challenging the core assumption of the disorganization theory that poor areas also suffer from a lack of social cohesion (Silva, 2014; Villareal & Silva, 2006). In El Salvador, I had observed where a transformed physical space created a safe, civil environment. I had also seen that a strong show of force contributed to that safe environment. Once I had placed these observations in the context of citizen security's origins in social disorganization, I realized that what was lacking was an examination of how policies and programs that intervene to improve the physical or social order of a neighborhood actually make a difference or fail to make a difference in the social life and security of those who live there.

CHAPTER 2

Methods and Hypothesis

With that in mind, I set out to describe both the physical and social order of two sets of neighborhoods in order to explore possible differences in social life and security. I describe the physical and social order of these neighborhoods as I observed over the course of numerous visits to gather archival sources, observe, and conduct interviews.

Archival data came from local newspapers, online resources, and municipal and other government records. For example, each municipality provided a copy of its citizen security plans and policies. I also obtained homicide data from law-enforcement agencies and the medical examiners' offices. Observations were conducted in all neighborhoods at various times of day and over the course of several visits. These archival and observational data provide greater context to the interview data, comprising both in-depth and survey interviews. The in-depth interviews were conducted with public officials, nongovernmental groups, and businesses in the case study neighborhoods. Similar to the archival and observation data, they provide greater context for the survey interviews.

The use of comparative neighborhood studies aligns the research with the work of the Chicago School theorists who first proposed disorganization theory. It also aligns the research with Robert Sampson's more recent work on collective efficacy. The research design mimics Sampson's purposeful use of a neighborhood as the unit of analysis and avoids the use of randomization given that randomization creates a "nonsocial" world (2012, p. x). Interviewing neighbors versus randomly selecting a sample of persons drawn from different neighborhoods provides a more complete picture of social life than if interviews were spread over a larger area. This approach pays more attention to "neighborhood effects" than to an aggregate of individual action or perceptions. As in the Chicago School tradition, neighborhoods are viewed in my research as both the consequence and cause, and the outcome and producer of social order.

With the complexity of neighborhood case studies in mind, my first priority in case selection was geography. All four case study neighborhoods are contiguous to the capital city of San Salvador in order to reduce major intervening variables such as rural–urban differences and drug routes or illegal commerce in outlying regions. The selection of the four cases was made in consultation with local experts and international agencies and based in part on access to communities (i.e., restrictions based on security). The process of community selection began with meetings in San Salvador and Washington, D.C., with community and municipal leaders, a local university, the U.S. Embassy, the U.S. Agency for International Development, the United Nations Office on Drugs and Crime, and various nongovernmental organizations. Follow-up conversations and visits were made with these resources to refine the list of communities.

Two of the case study neighborhoods are adjacent to *El Paseo* in the municipality of Santa Tecla. They have apparent physical order overall with better-kept public spaces, homes and buildings in decent repair, and less density. The other two neighborhoods are across the city in another suburb of San Salvador, Mejicanos. These two neighborhoods have fewer and less-well-maintained public spaces, more disrepair of homes and buildings, and greater density than the neighborhoods in Santa Tecla.

I selected these cases for various reasons. First, as we will see in the following chapters, the two municipalities offered interesting differences in crime and violence, land use, repair, housing stock, and demographics that have been used as indicators of social and physical order. Second, the pairs of adjacent neighborhoods also offered differences in physical order within the municipalities, creating a natural experiment to see if less-obvious indicators of social disorganization also existed. Finally, I had enough access to the neighborhoods to ensure security during my visits and the visits of survey enumerators. Access to communities without the introduction of a trusted source or where rival gangs operate would have been too risky. Given the exploratory nature of this research, the convenience sampling using the basic parameters above was enough to give me a sense of whether the disorganization hypothesis helps understand crime and violence in these neighborhoods.

The disorganization hypothesis would have us believe that the neighborhoods with more physical order will have less crime and violence than those with more physical disorder. However, it is possible that something else was going on in the neighborhoods that affected where crime and violence were occurring, something that could not be perceived through observation alone.

To determine if there was indeed something different in the social order between the neighborhoods, I collected survey-interview data on indicators of social order from disorganization theory, collective efficacy, and citizen security to try to tease out differences among the four neighborhoods. I looked at the various ways in which the communities come together for events and in organizations, how much neighbors trust and turn to one another for help, and the roles residents, businesses, and the municipality play in crime-prevention policy and programs.

If the world actually worked the way social scientists think it works, nicer-looking places would have many more community events, activities, and social occasions. People living in nicer-looking places would also face less crime and violence. Places that look deteriorated or rundown would have correspondingly fewer community events, a less active social life, and more crime and violence.

This means that the disorganization hypothesis has two sides. One is social, to be sure. The other is physical. The connection between the two is more than metaphorical. Policy makers, planners, and social reformers have long believed that fixing the way an area looks will not just affect what people do there but can actually make people act better. When planners propose changes to a neighborhood—by adding a park, for instance—they believe that the physical improvement to the space will elicit better behavior from residents and passers-by. They believe that the physical improvement can even make people think differently about themselves and one another. As shown in Table 1, where there is more "physical order," the disorganization hypothesis predicts that we will find more "social order." Where there is more "physical disorder," the hypothesis predicts that we will find more "social disorder." (I use the term "disorganization" to refer to the hypothesis, and the terms "order"/"disorder" when referring to the indicators of the hypothesis.)

Table 1. The Social Disorganization Hypothesis

	Physical order	Physical disorder
Social disorder		X
Social order	X	

In the following chapters, I use ideas from the physical side of the disorganization hypothesis to describe the case study neighborhoods. Based on indicators derived by other disorganization theorists, I characterized the neighborhoods as having "physical order" or "physical disorder" based first on their physical appearance. Using established indicators, I recorded how land was used and maintained, whether buildings were packed together or spread out, and how rundown the area's buildings looked (Greenberg, Rohe, & Williams, 1982; Kelling & Wilson,

1982; Park, 1915; Shaw, 1929; Shaw & McKay, 1942). I also based my categorization of physical disorder on each neighborhood's demographic characteristics. Like Louis Wirth (1938), I looked at the size, density, and heterogeneity of the population. Neighborhoods that had more people, more different kinds of people, and people more tightly packed were deemed to have more physical disorder.

Other groups of policy makers, planners, and social reformers have assumed that problems have less to do with the physical appearance of a neighborhood and more to do with the social side of the disorganization hypothesis. Thinkers on the social side propose programs that will help neighbors find more moments when they can come together and get along with one another. To reformers with this mindset, social problems are about not only a lack of civility or acting disrespectfully but also about the propensity of people to work together and confront shared challenges. Planners on the social side of the disorganization hypothesis seek to increase the amount of community and social life, or "social order," in a neighborhood. They increase the engagement and participation of residents by bringing them together in community events, neighborhood activities, and local organizations. I will also examine these indicators of social order in the case study neighborhoods in Chapter 5.

Policies that aim to reduce crime and violence in the case study neighborhoods are based on both the physical and social sides of the disorganization hypothesis. The policies seek to make neighborhoods look better so that the lives of the people who reside there will improve. They also seek to increase community engagement and participation. They do both of these things as ways to reduce or prevent crime and violence.

Unfortunately, it might not be that easy. As I detail in the following chapters, there is not always a one-to-one correspondence between physical disorder and crime. And, despite the various ways the literature provides to measure social order, I found little difference in the community and social life of the neighborhoods no matter the amount of physical disorder or crime. It would seem from these results that fixing the social order either directly through things like increased participation and community organization or indirectly with things like dressed-up public spaces might have less to do with crime and violence than the literature predicts.

As Sampson (2012) found in the United States, it appears that neighborhoods with physical disorder can have either social order or disorder, and neighborhoods with physical order can have either social order or disorder. There may not be as strong a correspondence as we think between the physical and social sides of disorganization. This means that fixes to the physical appearance of a neighborhood alone might not fix social problems such as crime and violence.

CHAPTER 3

Neighborhood Physical Order

All four case study neighborhoods are located in the Greater San Salvador metropolitan area (Figure 2). The adjacent neighborhoods of Santa Marta and Centro are located in the municipality of Santa Tecla to the west of San Salvador. The adjacent neighborhoods of San Ramon and Zacamil are located in the municipality of Mejicanos to the north of San Salvador.

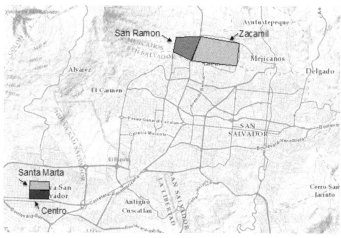

Figure 2. Location of neighborhoods in the San Salvador metropolitan area. (Source: Esri, 2014; author's rendering of neighborhood locations.)

Figure 3. Centro streetscape. (Source: author.)

To determine physical order or disorder of a neighborhood, theorists look at neighborhood environmental cues such as land use (Park, 1915; Park & Burgess, 1925), disrepair and abandonment (Kelling & Wilson, 1982), and types of streets and housing stock (Greenberg, Rohe, & Williams, 1982; Jacobs, 1961; Newman, 1972). I use these indicators of physical disorder to describe the case study neighborhoods in turn.

LAND USE

Land use was an early indicator employed to establish physical disorder. Robert Park (1915) summarized well the hypothesis linking land use to social disorder:

> The city is rooted in the habits and customs of the people who inhabit it. The consequence is that the city possesses a moral as well as a physical organization, and these two mutually interact in characteristic ways to mold and modify one another. (p. 578)

In these terms, the two case study neighborhoods in Santa Tecla—Centro and Santa Marta—have a unique location at the edge of San Salvador closest to ports and along a major highway. This is a strategic location for mixed-use development including light industry, free-trade zones, commercial services, and residential areas. Centro comprises mostly low, one-story stores and informal vendors concentrated in a market area close to the highway and across from an industrial area (Figure 3). Moving away from

the highway toward Santa Marta, the streetscape gives way to residential areas with a number of small shops operated out of current or converted homes.

The boundary between Centro and Santa Marta (Figure 4) contains two of the prized public uses of land in Santa Tecla—*Paseo del Carmen*, the commercial, pedestrian street at night and on weekends, and *El Cafetelón*, the large, rehabilitated park. On the other side of the pedestrian street, Santa Marta is a primarily residential neighborhood of one- and two-story single-family homes (Figure 5). A few small shops and offices operate out of some of the houses. Informal and formal food vendors line the street between the park and a large private high school in the neighborhood.

Figure 5. Santa Marta streetscape. (Source: author.)

The land use in the two case study neighborhoods in Mejicanos—
San Ramon and Zacamil—is primarily residential. In San Ramon,
residences are one-story, single-family homes, and storefronts are
mostly houses converted for business purposes (Figure 6). Vacant
lots and deteriorating walls dot the streetscape. Once surrounded
by farmland, some small industrial buildings are now visible at the
edges of the neighborhood, and the first Walmart in the country
occupies a large footprint at the edge of the neighborhood.

Just beyond the Walmart is Zacamil. There is little to distinguish
the neighborhoods at first. A few blocks into Zacamil, however, the

single-family homes give way to three- and four-story apartment buildings (Figure 7). There is little open space and no variation in building structure. There are some storefronts in homes but few other businesses apart from the central market area of the neighborhood. Here, informal vendors surround the municipal market building.

The recent rehabilitation of two parks, one in Santa Tecla between the case study neighborhoods (Figure 8) and one in Mejicanos, next to Zacamil (Figure 9), offers perhaps the most vivid contrast between the two municipalities in terms of physical order. In interviews with public officials at both locations, I learned that both rehabilitation projects sought to provide spaces for community members to come together and to provide recreational opportunities for youth. Given its location and buy-in from businesses and municipal government, the park in Santa Tecla is used often for everything from community yoga to soccer games. Meanwhile, I learned, the park in Mejicanos is often vacant or used only for pickup games of soccer. The level and threats of violence against those who would use it is too great for regular use of the open space. Instead, a neighboring community center is the site of most municipal programming, given the ability to vet participants and police the indoor space.

Figure 9. Rehabilitated park near Zacamil. (Source: author.)

DISREPAIR AND ABANDONMENT

The next set of physical disorder indicators consider how rundown a neighborhood looks. The idea that disrepair and abandonment are indicators of physical disorder that lead to social disorder such as crime is summarized well in the "broken windows" theory. George Kelling and James Wilson (1982), who first established the theory, noted:

> . . . At the community level, disorder and crime are usually inextricably linked, in a kind of developmental sequence. Social psychologists and police officers tend to agree that if a window in a building is broken and is left unrepaired, all the rest of the windows will soon be broken. This is as true in nice neighborhoods as in rundown ones. . . . One unrepaired broken window is a signal that no one cares, and so breaking more windows costs nothing. (pp. 31–32)

In terms of disrepair and abandonment, the Centro neighborhood has older buildings with peeling paint in the commercial area. A large, partially collapsed building stands prominently on one edge of the central plaza (Figure 10). Some trash is strewn about, but the area is mostly well kept. In the residential area, the streets are lined with well-maintained cement block homes behind walls topped with barbed wire. The streets are pot-holed, sidewalks uneven, and paint peels from walls, but there is little trash.

Figure 10. Disrepair in Centro. (Source: author.)

The *El Paseo* pedestrian area and adjoining park are by far the most well kept parts of the Centro and Santa Marta neighborhoods. The street, sidewalks, and streetlights along *El Paseo* are new, and storefronts are freshly painted. The state of repair of the Santa Marta neighborhood is similar to that of Centro's residential streets, with relatively fewer pot holes and better-maintained walls and gates. Behind the walls, homes in Santa Marta have newer paint and more trees.

In San Ramon and Mejicanos, the disrepair and abandonment are more acute. Looking down at the neighborhood of San Ramon from a vantage point on the skirt of the San Salvador volcano, one sees primarily corrugated metal roofs; numerous overgrown, vacant lots; and some dirt and gravel streets. Where streets are paved, they tend to be pot-holed, but in passable condition (Figure 11). There is little trash on the streets or sidewalks, but accumulations in vacant lots are common. Moving down the volcano and closer to Zacamil, one sees streets between homes become narrow alleyways with dirt footpaths.

In Zacamil, the multi-family residential buildings are worn, and paint is peeling. Walls and lamp posts are covered with graffiti and old advertisements. The streets are mostly clean, but trash accumulates in some gutters.

Figure 11. Disrepair in San Ramon. (Source: author.)

STREET TYPE AND HOUSING STOCK

The final set of indicators of physical disorder includes a neighborhood's streets and houses. Greenberg, Rohe, and Williams (1982) summarize the hypothesized link between these indicators of physical disorder and social disorder:

> The more the street design is able to delineate public and private areas, the greater its effectiveness in reducing crime. A street design that accommodates large numbers of those living outside the neighborhood increases both the number of potential victims and the number of potential offenders in the neighborhood. (p. 143)

In these terms, the highway that enters the Centro neighborhood brings a large number of outsiders through it. A great deal of pedestrian and vehicle traffic mixes together along the sides of the highway and in the midst of informal vendors and bus stops. Once in the residential area, one finds the streets have become more private until one arrives at the pedestrian mall and park. Both public areas attract a large number of outsiders during the day and, along the pedestrian mall, at night, when bars stay open late. On the other side of the pedestrian mall, in Santa Marta, there is much less vehicle traffic than in Centro, and some of the streets are empty apart from the parked cars. Public buses headed for the center of San Salvador frequent a couple of streets.

Table 2. Infrastructure Indicators of Physical Disorder

	Physical order (Santa Tecla)	Physical disorder (Mejicanos)
	CENTRO	ZACAMIL
Land use	-	-
Disrepair/abandonment	-/+	-/+
Street and housing type	-/+	-
	SANTA MARTA	SAN RAMON
Land use	+	-/+
Disrepair/abandonment	+	-
Street and housing type	+	+

Note: (-) indicates negative cues, (+) indicates positive cues, (-/+) indicates presence of both.

Across town, in San Ramon, a new ring road ends in front of the Walmart, increasing the amount of external visitors to the once-remote neighborhood. Within the neighborhood, there is mostly local foot traffic and very little vehicle traffic on the residential streets and in alleyways. Just off the main road between San Ramon and Zacamil is the end of a major bus route that brings a number of outsiders to the communities. Streets in Zacamil are narrow and winding, with light vehicle and pedestrian traffic.

Finally, the housing stock of each neighborhood is theorized to play a part in its level of organization (Newman, 1972). Both the Centro and Santa Marta neighborhoods are composed of mainly one- or two-story single-family homes. The homes in the Santa Marta neighborhood are bigger and have larger yards within their walls.

The houses in San Ramon are similar to those of Santa Marta, but more modest in terms of size and building materials. They are more often left unpainted, and the high walls seen near Centro and Santa Marta are less ubiquitous. Housing in Zacamil comprises row after row of multi-family apartment buildings. The single-story single-family homes that do exist are in poor condition.

Table 2 summarizes the indicators of physical disorder described above. Using observations of each neighborhood based on these indicators, I found that San Ramon and Zacamil have greater physical disorder than Centro and Santa Marta. This finding is based largely on the fact that Zacamil comprises mainly multi-family units and the fact that it and San Ramon have more disrepair.

The physical characteristics are but one aspect of physical disorder. To more fully describe the physical disorder beyond appearance alone, theorists suggest that we must know more about the type and variety of people who inhabit the neighborhoods. For them, physical disorder includes not only the landscape of a neighborhood but also the varieties of people who inhabit that landscape. A classic example is Louis Wirth (1938), a contemporary of Shaw and McKay, who noted that size, density, and heterogeneity are the basic facts necessary for understanding a neighborhood. More recently, in their test of the social disorganization hypothesis, Sampson and Groves (1989) echoed and expanded Wirth's characteristics. They included variables such as economic status, residential mobility, and family disruption.

Data on the demographic elements of physical disorder in El Salvador are available only down to the municipal level. As shown in Table 3, when we examine the demographic predictors we find further justification for the categorization of greater levels of disorder in Mejicanos (San Ramon and Zacamil) when compared with Santa Tecla (Centro and Santa Marta).

Table 3 shows that economic status, as measured by per capita gross domestic product, is roughly the same in both municipalities. The rate of home ownership, often an indicator of mobility, is also nearly the same. There is a difference in mobility as measured by recent arrivals, however. There were twice as many recent arrivals in Santa Tecla as in Mejicanos. Recent arrivals could have come from the next block over or from a different part of the country; there is no way to know with the available data. Despite these new arrivals, there was a net population loss in both municipalities, largely because of emigration out of the country (*Dirección General de Estadísticas y Censos* [DIGESTYC], 2007).

Table 3. Demographic Indicators of Physical Disorder

Municipality (neighborhoods)	GDP per capita	Own home	Recent arrival[a]	Population[b]	Population change[c]	Population density
Mejicanos (Zacamil/San Ramon)	$11,939	70.1%	8.41%	140,751	-2.9%	6,363/mi^2
Santa Tecla (Centro/Santa Marta)	$12,455	71.8%	16.25%	108,840	-6.3%	1,087/mi^2

Notes: [a] *Arrived between 1997 and 2007.* [b] *2007, urban areas only.* [c] *1992–2007. Sources: Dirección General de Estadística y Censos DIGESTYC, 2007; UNDP, 2009d.*

The greatest difference between the two municipalities is population density. Even when we consider only the urban areas of the municipalities (Santa Tecla also includes a large rural area), Mejicanos has nearly six times the density of Santa Tecla. As we saw above, this is due in large part to the multi-family apartment buildings around Zacamil and similar communities in the municipality. Greater population density is an indicator of physical disorder.

Wirth's idea of ethnic heterogeneity is less of an issue in either community or in El Salvador generally. There are very few foreign populations in El Salvador, and none of any appreciable size. While there is an historical distinction between indigenous (darker-skinned) and *mestizo* (lighter-skinned) populations, ethnic heterogeneity is less prevalent in urban areas of El Salvador today than it was in the United States in the mid-twentieth century. In any case, no census data distinguish ethnicity, demonstrating the lack of significance it has compared with ethnic relations in Sampson and Groves's work on physical disorder in Chicago.

Similarly, Sampson and Groves's concept of family disruption is difficult to replicate or apply with available census data. Formal marriage is less common in El Salvador than in the United States, so the use of rates of single parenthood might be skewed. In any case, the data indicate no difference between the two municipalities in terms of single-parent families, at approximately one-third of all homes in both Mejicanos and Santa Tecla (DIGESTYC, 2007). We also know that migration and violence have contributed to family disruption, often resulting in the absence of one or both parents (UNDP, 2005). As we saw above, the amount of population decline is equal in both Santa Tecla and Mejicanos.

The demographic data on the neighborhoods suggest that, overall, the neighborhoods in Mejicanos have more physical disorder than in Santa Tecla, especially given the population density in the municipality. An examination of all of the data on physical disorder together—both appearance and demographics—suggests that more physical disorder is found in Mejicanos, which includes the case study neighborhoods of San Ramon and Zacamil. More physical order is found in Santa Tecla, which includes the case study neighborhoods of Centro and Santa Marta.

CHAPTER 4

Neighborhood Crime and Violence

The second task is to categorize the neighborhoods using data on the amount of crime and violence in each area. I was particularly interested to see how crime and violence, as the key indicator of interest, related to the physical order observed in the neighborhoods. First, certain distinctions had to be kept in mind about the way crime and violence were measured. There are two main approaches. One is the amount of crime and violence observed and reported in the data. The other is the perception of crime. The disorganization hypothesis has traditionally focused on observed crime rates. In debating disorganization, theorists most often refer to data on such things as homicide and victimization. Meanwhile, proponents of citizen security emphasize the perceptions of crime and violence, referring to people's "sense of security." In order to have a complete picture of crime in the case study neighborhoods, I examine both observed crime and perceptions of crime. All three indicators—sense of security, homicide rate, and victimization rate—are used here to categorize neighborhoods as having "more crime" or "less crime."

In 2010, the national homicide rate in El Salvador was 65.4 per 100,000 (*Instituto de Medicina Legal* [IML], 2010). As Table 4 shows, Mejicanos (which includes San Ramon and Zacamil) had a higher homicide rate than the national average in 2010, and Santa Tecla (which includes Santa Marta and Centro) had a much lower rate than the average. The trends show an increase for Mejicanos, where the homicide rate more than doubled in ten years. The trend in Santa Tecla is downward, with less than half the number of homicides compared with a decade earlier.

Table 4. Homicides and Homicide Rates

		Homicide rate trend		
	Homicides[a]	2000	2005	2010
Santa Tecla	29	52.4	49.3	22.1
Santa Marta	0			
Centro	3			
Mejicanos	105	27.7	44.4	68.3
San Ramon	3			
Zacamil	9			

Notes: [a] *Latest available year. Sources: Municipal totals and Mejicanos neighborhoods from* IML, *2011; Santa Tecla neighborhoods from* Observatorio Municipal para la Prevención de la Violencia/PNC, *2012.*

Table 4 also shows that the number of homicides varies between neighborhoods within the same municipality. It comes as no surprise that homicides are not evenly distributed in a municipality. Based on number of homicides alone, Zacamil and Centro are the neighborhoods with greater levels of violence relative to San Ramon and Santa Marta respectively.

These raw data are imperfect, however, and several issues arise when comparing neighborhood homicide data. Homicides that occur in adjoining neighborhoods or even across a neighborhood boundary may be counted elsewhere despite their impact on all surrounding communities. There is also the challenge of reliability at the local level. Official police and medical examiner statistics are often inaccurate. For example, the police reported twenty-five homicides in Santa Tecla in 2010, while the medical examiner reported twenty-nine in the same year. Crime and violence statistics such as these are notoriously unreliable in Latin America (Bergman, 2006). This is especially true at the neighborhood level, given errors in data collection and variability in reporting between precincts. For instance, the police might record where a homicide occurred while the coroner might report where the body was examined, even in a hospital across town from where the homicide occurred. Homicide statistics are especially dubious in El Salvador recently given the increasing prevalence of "disappearances" (Wells, 2013). For example, in order to demonstrate progress on a truce between gangs that occurred during my observations, gang members turned to creating mass graves to dispose of bodies. If there was no body, the thinking went, then the official statistics cannot list a homicide that would have put the truce in jeopardy.

VICTIMIZATION RATES

In any case, homicide statistics alone do not tell the whole story. It is not just homicides that make a neighborhood unsafe and communities feel insecure (Cruz & Santacruz Giralt, 2005). Other crimes such as robberies, car theft, rape, assaults, and extortion, which often go unreported, along with the presence or absence of gangs, are important indicators of a neighborhood's security. One alternative that researchers use to capture that information is a victimization survey. A victimization survey is often more reliable than official data for the reasons listed above, and given that many crimes go unreported because of a lack of trust in police (Labrador & Sanz, 2012). Official data may be skewed as more crimes could be reported in areas where people trust the police, and fewer crimes could be reported in areas where people do not trust the police. Thus, one area would appear to have more crime only because there is more trust in police, when that might not be the case.

One example of the crime-reporting challenge comes from an interviewee in San Ramon, who noted that she and her small business had been victimized by extortion. Extortion of businesses of all sizes and types is common in many neighborhoods around San Salvador and is most often perpetrated by gangs with threats of violence against the owner, staff, and their families. A note signed by a local gang was left in this woman's business requesting that $500 be placed in a bag and left outside at a certain time. The business owner was frightened but did not immediately call the police. She showed the note to colleagues and discussed possible options, including how to obtain the requested funds. During the course of these discussions, it became clearer to the owner that the threat might not have come from a gang. The note had been found inside the business, and no one could recall seeing an unknown person in the preceding days. The handwritten note also had a familiar script. The owner decided it could have come from a recently dismissed employee seeking revenge. She took her chances, filling a bag with paper and placing it outside at the appointed hour. She had a friend watch the location to see who picked up the bag. In the end, the bag was delivered to the last known address of the disgruntled employee. While no physical harm had been done, the business owner and her staff were left shaken and scrutinized everyone who came and left more closely. Because this extortion was not reported to the police, it does not figure in official statistics. It is, however, representative of the victimization that occurs frequently and is difficult to capture and quantify across the neighborhoods.

Using rates of victimization as a proxy for all crime in a neighborhood, however, opens the door to other inaccuracies of reporting, such as an interviewee's fear of mentioning a crime and a lack of ability to verify. Thus, researchers often ask if an interviewee knows of a neighbor who has been victimized. This allows for a degree of anonymity and distance in mentioning a crime. That is what I did in the survey interviews conducted in the neighborhoods, leaving open the possibility that interviewees might expand on an experience as the extorted business owner did.

Using the survey-interview data, Table 5 shows the rates of victimization in each of the case study neighborhoods. As we can see, San Ramon and Centro have higher rates of victimization overall, but as the frequency of victimization increases, Zacamil and Centro show greater incidence of victimization.

Table 5. Victimization Rates

	Victimization	Frequency	
		1–2 events	*3+ events*
Santa Tecla			
Santa Marta	40%	65.0%	35.0%
Centro	51%	18.2%	81.8%
Mejicanos			
San Ramon	52%	65.4%	34.6%
Zacamil	44%	54.5%	45.5%

Note: Question = "In the last year, has anyone you know been the victim of a crime in this neighborhood?" Source: Author's survey-interview data (N=194).

The type of crime also varies by neighborhood, with violent crimes (sexual assault, homicide, armed robbery) reported with greater frequency than nonviolent crimes (car theft, home burglary, robbery, or assault) in Centro (91 percent of victims) compared with Santa Marta (50 percent of victims), and Zacamil (50 percent of victims) compared with San Ramon (38 percent of victims). According to Labrador & Sanz (2012), these higher levels of violent victimization are an accurate reflection of greater amounts of crime and violence in Zacamil and Centro compared with San Ramon and Santa Marta, respectively.

SENSE OF SECURITY

Still, as citizen security proponents claim, one can feel safe in a neighborhood with a lot of homicides and where neighbors are victimized. Someone else can feel unsafe in a neighborhood with less crime. To account for these discrepancies, citizen security draws especially on the reported sense of security in a neighborhood (Guerrero Velasco et al., 2012).

Sense of security is often used a proxy for observed rates of crime and violence given the deficiencies in those data described above. It is especially important for the present research for two additional reasons. First, it is a primary indicator of citizen security and it most closely reflects the expectations for control in collective efficacy. While rates of crime and violence can also be used, they do not tell us about the expectations or perceptions of community members regarding crime in their neighborhoods. Second, a sense of insecurity, not experienced victimization or crime, has been the primary problem in the country cited by Salvadorans responding to national polls over the past few years (Latin American Public Opinion Project, 2010; Segura, 2013).

An initial review of the survey-interview data confirms that the same is true in all of the case study communities as shown in Table 6. At least two-thirds of respondents in every neighborhood saw insecurity as the greatest problem their community confronts. Just how insecure and how much that insecurity has changed over time varied by neighborhood, however. In Centro and Zacamil, respondents felt more insecure more of the time. They also did not feel much safer than they did five years earlier. Meanwhile, respondents in Santa Marta and San Ramon felt more secure more of the time when compared with Centro and Zacamil, and more of them felt comparatively safer over time.

Table 6. Sense of Security

	Insecurity as greatest problem	Feel very or somewhat safe	Always feel safe	Feel safer than 5 years ago
Santa Tecla				
Santa Marta	66.9%	95.2%	59.1%	50.0%
Centro	97.7%	90.7%	11.1%	2.3%
Mejicanos				
San Ramon	66.0%	88%	40%	10%
Zacamil	75.8%	79.5%	30%	4.1%

Source: Author's survey-interview data ("Problem" N=191, all others N=194).

It is worth noting that across all neighborhoods, the primary drivers of increased sense of security reported by interviewees were activities for youth (28 percent) and police or military patrols (27 percent). The primary drivers of decreased sense of security were lack of employment opportunities (34 percent) and lack of educational opportunities (20 percent). Indicators of social and physical disorganization such as trust (7 percent) and public spaces (3 percent) were not cited as much.

To summarize the data on crime and violence presented above: Zacamil and Centro have more homicides, greater incidence of victimization, and less sense of security relative to their adjacent neighborhoods. They are therefore classified as the neighborhoods with "more crime" while San Ramon and Santa Marta are classified as the neighborhoods with "less crime." (When referring to these classifications of neighborhoods, I use "crime" as shorthand for "crime and violence.")

NEIGHBORHOOD CRIME AND PHYSICAL ORDER

Based on all of the observations and data presented thus far, we now have the four case study neighborhoods categorized by physical disorder and crime as shown in Table 7.

Table 7. Neighborhoods by Crime and Physical Order

	Physical order (Santa Tecla)	Physical disorder (Mejicanos)
More crime	Centro	Zacamil
Less crime	Santa Marta	San Ramon

As shown in Table 7, the neighborhoods of Zacamil and San Ramon are classified as areas of physical disorder. In these neighborhoods, the data showed greater population density and I observed more multi-family units and general disrepair. These are all indicators of physical disorder according to the literature.

The neighborhoods of Centro and Zacamil are classified as areas with more crime. In these neighborhoods, the data showed more homicides, greater incidence of victimization, and less sense of security. These are all indicators of greater amounts of crime and violence according to the literature.

Despite what the disorganization hypothesis predicted, the data suggest that indicators of social disorder such as crime can differ even within areas that share the same amount of physical disorder. As shown at the outset (Table 1), the disorganization hypothesis predicted that the neighborhoods of physical order, Santa Marta and Centro, would both fall into the "less crime" category. It also predicted that the neighborhoods of physical disorder, San Ramon and Zacamil, would both fall into the "more crime" category. To the contrary, it seems that areas with similar amounts of physical disorder can have different amounts of social disorder. Areas with different amounts of physical disorder can have similar amounts of social disorder. This bears restating: There is reason to be suspicious of the disorganization hypothesis at this point. There is already no one-to-one correspondence between the physical and social sides of the hypothesis.

This should not come as a surprise, as this is not the first time these suspicions have been raised. The physical side of disorganization was called into question almost as soon as it came into being. Evidence was produced from Boston that rundown areas could exhibit high levels of social order and control problems such as crime (Gans, 1962; Suttles, 1968; Whyte, 1943). Later, in St. Louis, suburbs with a great deal of physical order were found to have social order problems such as gangs and delinquency that were previously assumed to occur only in dense urban areas (Monti, 1994). Finally, in Chicago, the physical disorder of a neighborhood was found to be less predictive of problems than the amount of social control exhibited by its residents (Sampson, 2012). It appears that the analysis to this point aligns with these previous findings from across the United States.

This is just the beginning of the analysis, however. People have come up with three ways to elaborate upon and tease out the correspondence between physical and social disorder. Each is associated with different but complementary sets of indicators. First are the indicators of social order beyond crime and violence, such as the community and social life in a neighborhood, which complete the disorganization hypothesis. Then there are the indicators from theories that draw on disorganization, namely collective efficacy and citizen security. An analysis of the correspondence between each set of social indicators and physical disorder and crime and violence follows in Chapter 5. Those data are not widely available for most neighborhoods. A great deal of legwork went into acquiring the social indicators, and that effort is why the physical side is often used alone—it is much easier to observe, even though it may not always be accurate.

Neighborhood Social Disorder

As we have seen, social scientists and policy makers on the physical side of disorganization theory argue that one can predict the kind of social life people have and how much crime they face based on how their neighborhood looks. For them, nicer-looking places would have many more neighborhood events, social activities, and community organizations. People living in nicer-looking places would also experience less crime and violence in their neighborhood. Places that look deteriorated or rundown would have correspondingly fewer community events, a less active social life, and more crime and violence. Policy makers on the physical side of the disorganization hypothesis seek to improve "physical order," or way a place looks, by cleaning it up, fixing up rundown buildings and streets, and adding public spaces such as parks.

Other groups of social scientists and policy makers have assumed that problems have less to do with the physical appearance of a neighborhood and more to do with the social side of the disorganization hypothesis. They propose programs that will help neighbors get along better with one another and come together more often. To reformers with this mindset, social problems are not only about a lack of civility or acting disrespectfully. They are also about the propensity of people to work together and confront shared challenges. Policy makers on the social side of the disorganization hypothesis seek to directly increase the amount of community and social life, or "social order," in a neighborhood. They increase the engagement and participation of residents by bringing them together in neighborhood events, social activities, and organizations. Indicators of social order also include things like events, activities, and organizations. Additionally, proponents argue that you can also look at whether newcomers are integrated into the community, how much and how often people come together, and how much neighbors trust one another and whether they share the same values. All of these indicators elaborate upon the correspondence between physical and social order.

I examine these indicators in the case study neighborhoods and will also see whether there is correspondence between the various indicators on the social side and crime and violence. In this second analysis for each set of indicators, I will see if policy makers who focus on fixing the social side of disorganization in an effort to reduce crime and violence are on better footing than those on the physical side.

To analyze the correspondence between physical and social order, and social order and crime and violence, I asked people in the case study neighborhoods about things like integrating newcomers, attending events and meetings of various organizations, and how much or little cohesion there is among their neighbors. From more than 200 survey interviews and in-depth key informant interviews in the neighborhoods, I found that, overall, people answered the questions similarly no matter whether they lived in a nice-looking or rundown neighborhood, or a neighborhood with more or less crime and violence. Contrary to the disorganization hypothesis, there was little to no difference in community and social life no matter the amount of physical disorder or crime. In the following sections I try to tease out any differences that might not be apparent at first. I examine the correspondence between each indicator and physical disorder, and then between each indicator and crime and violence.

According to the disorganization hypothesis, the neighborhoods with physical order should have more responses indicating social order than the neighborhoods with physical disorder. The case study neighborhoods of Centro and Santa Marta should have greater social order than those of Zacamil and San Ramon. There should be more indications of cohesion and engagement in nicer neighborhoods and fewer in rundown neighborhoods. What we would expect to see in Figure 12 are the first two bars in each cluster, representing neighborhoods with physical order, rising higher than the second two, representing neighborhoods with physical disorder.

The first indicator, whether people perceive their neighborhood to be tight-knit or not, shows the greatest difference between physically ordered and disordered neighborhoods. In the nicer-looking neighborhoods of Santa Marta and Centro, more people agreed with the idea that their neighborhood was tight-knit than in the deteriorating neighborhoods. When asked whether people trust their neighbors, there was also a difference between neighborhoods with physical order and neighborhoods with physical disorder. These results are in line with the disorganization hypothesis. On the question of whether people in the neighborhood share the same values, however, the results were mixed. One nicer-looking neighborhood, Centro, fell far below both rundown neighborhoods.

Overall, the first three indicators show little support for the hypothesis. Some amount of cohesion may vary between neighborhoods based on their physical order, but that does not translate into greater trust or shared values. As we saw in the literature, trust and cohesion might matter, but it is what people do with that cohesion that is most important. Even if people perceive some amount of closeness with their neighbors, their behavior is what matters most for social control. The last three indicators focus on those behaviors.

When we examine the behaviors of respondents, again we find mixed results or no difference between neighborhoods. In both

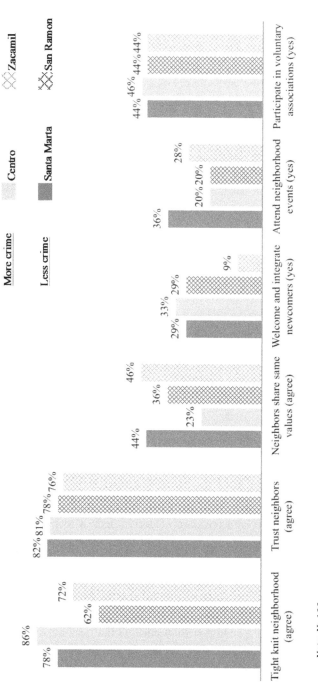

Figure 12. Indicators of Social Order

Note: N=193.

nicer-looking neighborhoods and one rundown neighborhood, San Ramon, people reportedly welcomed and integrated newcomers at about the same rate. One of the neighborhoods of physical disorder, Zacamil, fell well below all the others. That part of the result is in line with the disorganization hypothesis. The same is true of the question of whether people attend neighborhood events. Part of the result is in line with the hypothesis while another is not. People attend events more in Santa Marta than in either rundown neighborhood. They attend fewer events in Centro than in Zacamil and at about the same number as in San Ramon. The last indicator, participation in voluntary associations, shows little difference no matter the physical appearance and demographics of the neighborhood.

These mixed and small differences provide little support for the disorganization hypothesis. It appears from these data that there are few areas of correspondence between the social and physical sides of the hypothesis in these neighborhoods. Apart from a small difference in cohesion and trust, people in nicer-looking areas do not appear to think about one another or engage with one another much differently from the way people in less-appealing places do.

CORRESPONDENCE BETWEEN SOCIAL DISORDER, CRIME, AND VIOLENCE

The disorganization hypothesis also predicts that we will find a difference in social order between neighborhoods that have more and less crime and violence. There should be more indications of cohesion and engagement in neighborhoods with less crime and violence, and fewer in neighborhoods with more crime and violence. The case study neighborhoods of Santa Marta and San Ramon should have greater social order than Centro and Zacamil. Looking again at Figure 12, we would expect to see the darker bars for each indicator rising higher than the lighter pair of bars. Santa Marta should be higher than Centro (solid bars), and San Ramon should be higher than Zacamil (hatched bars).

The first indicator, whether people perceive their neighborhood to be tight-knit or not, shows the greatest difference between neighborhoods. However, that difference goes against the hypothesis. In the neighborhoods with more crime—Centro and Zacamil—more people agreed with the idea that their neighborhood was tight-knit than in the neighborhoods with less crime. Meanwhile, the amount of trust respondents had in their neighbors was in line with the disorganization hypothesis. More people trust their neighbors in the less-crime neighborhoods of Santa Marta and San Ramon than in the adjacent more-crime neighborhoods of Centro and Zacamil.

Trust is a major topic that any visitor to Central America will note after a few conversations, and a theme that ran through many interviews. In a postconflict society with major economic inequalities, interpersonal trust does not come easily. In interviews and conversations, "*no hay confianza . . .* " or "I don't trust . . . " came up frequently even for the most mundane of interactions such as about from whom to purchase basic goods. Given those discussions, it is somewhat surprising that greater than three-quarters of respondents in each neighborhood said they had trust in their neighbors. More surprising, for all the talk of whether someone can be trusted, is that trust does not differ no matter the level of crime and violence or physical order.

The perception that neighbors shared the same values was mixed. One less-crime neighborhood, Santa Marta, did surpass its more-crime neighborhood. The other less-crime neighborhood, San Ramon, fell well below its more-crime neighborhood. It appears there is little correspondence to support the disorganization hypothesis in these cases between either cohesion and crime or shared values and crime in these neighborhoods. The level of trust in neighbors appears to correspond better to the hypothesis. From these three indicators, we see that the perceptions of relationships between neighbors have some, but not much, correspondence with the amount of crime and violence in a neighborhood.

Again, the last three indicators look at the behaviors of respondents. They examine whether or not they engage with their neighbors no matter how they perceive their relationships. The difference between welcoming and integrating newcomers was mixed. One neighborhood with less crime, Santa Marta, fell below its more-crime neighborhood, while the other less-crime neighborhood, San Ramon, was well above its more crime pair. The fact that the neighborhood with more crime and physical disorder (Zacamil) had very low reported integration of newcomers supports the disorganization hypothesis. However, the results are inconsistent across all the neighborhoods. There is little correspondence between crime and violence and social order as measured by these indicators.

The same is true about whether people attend neighborhood events. Here, however, the neighborhood with less crime and physical order, Santa Marta, had the highest level of attendance, as the hypothesis predicts. Meanwhile, the neighborhood with more crime and physical disorder, Zacamil, had greater attendance than its pair with less crime, San Ramon. So we see inconsistency yet again in the results. The lack of correspondence continues with the final indicator of participation in voluntary associations. There was almost no variation in participation among the neighborhoods, no matter the amount of crime.

These data do little to show the differences we would expect between the social side of the disorganization hypothesis in areas with more and less crime. Apart from trusting their neighbors, people in areas of less crime such as the neighborhoods of Santa Marta and San Ramon do not appear to think about one another or engage with one another much differently from people in places with more crime such as Centro and Zacamil. It appears from these data that policy makers who focus on fixing the social side of disorganization in an effort to reduce crime in these neighborhoods are on no better footing than those on the physical side.

CORRESPONDENCE BETWEEN COLLECTIVE EFFICACY AND PHYSICAL ORDER

Similar to disorganization theory, collective efficacy hypothesizes that neighborhoods with physical order should have more responses indicating social order than the neighborhoods with physical disorder. There should be more indications of getting along and exhibiting social control in nicer neighborhoods such as Santa Marta and Centro, and fewer in rundown neighborhoods such as San Ramon and Zacamil.

As in the previous analysis, what we would expect to see in Figure 13 are the first two bars for each indicator, representing neighborhoods with physical order, being taller than the second two, representing neighborhoods with physical disorder.

Some differences in the first two indicators align with collective efficacy theory. As the theory predicts, the nicer-looking neighborhoods (Santa Marta and Centro) are where we find more people getting along with one another, and more people willing to help their neighbors. This is somewhat true as well for whether people get involved to solve neighborhood problems, but that correspondence is not as consistent. One nicer-looking neighborhood (Santa Marta) reports much more willingness to get involved than any of the other neighborhoods. Meanwhile, the other nicer-looking neighborhood (Centro) reports the same or less willingness to get involved than the rundown areas (San Ramon and Zacamil). Collective efficacy does a better job so far at teasing out the differences in social order between nicer- and not-so-nice-looking neighborhoods than did other indicators on the social side of disorganization.

The remaining indicators in Figure 13 look at the behaviors of respondents in collective efficacy theory. These indicators examine whether neighbors actually turn to one another and the authorities for help, no matter how much they think they get along with one another or think they would help one another. When it comes to behaviors like turning to neighbors for assistance or directly intervening, the results show little correspondence with physical order. One nicer neighborhood (Santa Marta) fell well below all the other neighborhoods in seeking assistance and directly intervening, while the other nicer neighborhood (Centro) was in line with the rundown neighborhoods. Contrary to the theory, the physical appearance of a neighborhood appears to have little to do with how neighbors get involved in their communities.

Physical order does, however, correspond better to the last indicator, whether the police are called to report a crime.

Figure 13. Indicators of Collective Efficacy

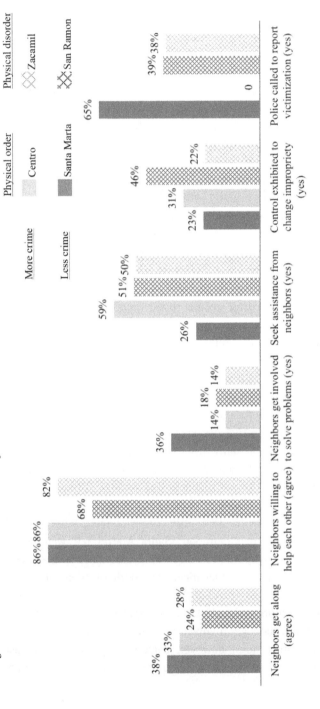

Notes: "Seek assistance" = Neighbors as first or second choice from whom to seek assistance among options of family, neighbors, church, municipality, or local organization/association. "Police called" in Centro = 0 due to case loss in response to knowing victim in neighborhood. N=193.

The nicer neighborhood (Santa Marta) shows a substantial difference in reporting crime to the authorities than the rundown neighborhoods. Even though there is no correspondence between direct intervention by neighbors and a neighborhood's appearance, there may be something to the correspondence between a neighborhood's appearance and its exhibiting control by calling the authorities.

Taken together, the indicators of collective efficacy show that the perceptions of social control have more correspondence with the physical appearance and demographics of a neighborhood than did observed behavior. That is not completely unexpected, as Sampson (2012) hypothesized that perceptions matter more than reality when it comes to social control. The indicators of collective efficacy were also able to tease out more correspondence with physical order overall than the indicators of the social side of disorganization. People in nicer-looking areas such as Santa Marta and Centro think about helping one another more than people in less-appealing places such as San Ramon and Zacamil. Notably, however, they do not appear to actually engage in helping one another much differently from people in less-appealing places.

CORRESPONDENCE BETWEEN COLLECTIVE EFFICACY, CRIME, AND VIOLENCE

Collective efficacy theory also predicts that we will find a correspondence between indicators of social order and crime and violence. There should be more indications of neighbors' getting along and exhibiting social control in neighborhoods with less crime and violence, and fewer in neighborhoods with more crime and violence. Looking again at Figure 13, we would expect to see the darker bars for each indicator above their lighter pair. Santa Marta should be higher than Centro (solid bars), and San Ramon should be higher than Zacamil (hatched bars).

The first two indicators, neighbors' getting along and helping one another, show little difference no matter the amount of crime in a neighborhood. Where there is a difference (between San

Ramon and Zacamil), in both cases that difference runs contrary to the theory. In Zacamil, the neighborhood with more crime, the perception is stronger that neighbors get along and are willing to help one another than in San Ramon, the neighborhood with less crime. When it comes to neighbors' getting involved to solve problems, the third indicator, there is greater correspondence with crime. People in areas with less crime think that their neighbors are more willing to get involved to solve problems. This provides some evidence of correspondence between perceptions of social control and amount of crime in a neighborhood. Again to this point, collective efficacy does a marginally better job of teasing out differences in the social order between neighborhoods with more and less crime than did the indicators of social disorganization.

Once again, however, the results for indicators that measure the actual behavior of neighbors show less correspondence or run contrary to the theory. Seeking the assistance of a neighbor is much less likely in the less-crime neighborhood of Santa Marta than it is in the more-crime neighborhood of Centro, for example. In the other two neighborhoods it is nearly the same no matter the amount of crime and violence. Exhibiting social control to change impropriety is less frequent again in the relatively low-crime area of Santa Marta than in higher-crime Centro. Meanwhile, the opposite is true in the other two neighborhoods. There is more control exhibited in less-crime San Ramon than in more-crime Zacamil, a partial finding in support of the theory. Finally, exhibiting control by calling the police shows little difference in the more- and less-crime neighborhoods for which data are available.

The reason for the lack of consistency in calling the police to report crime is illustrated by interviewees who, when asked if crimes in the neighborhood were reported to police, responded, "No, it's not worth it." In a follow-up, one interviewee noted the number of times he had called the police and they never arrived. Now, he says, he doesn't even bother. Even if interviewees had more trust in police, the chance that a perpetrator would be caught and convicted of a crime is small. For example, the Ministry of Justice and Security of El Salvador reported that a perpetrator is convicted in only 4 percent of homicides (Labrador & Sanz, 2012). More likely, in the respondents' eyes, the perpetrator or their associates will come back and retaliate against the person who reported the crime.

This near-universal impunity undermines collective efficacy theory. Whether or not people call the police may be only partially dependent on their willingness to intervene to help someone in need, as the theory hypothesizes. They may be willing to intervene by calling the police but see no value in doing so. Sampson himself predicted this problem for collective efficacy in the countries of Latin America (2012, p. 167). With high levels of impunity, a history of police corruption, and uneven adherence to the rule of law, the region is a unique testing ground for the theory.

Similarly, whether or not people will intervene on behalf of a victim may also depend on their perception of the likelihood of retaliation. Among those respondents who stated that the police were not called when someone was victimized in the neighborhood, the majority in all neighborhoods cited fear of retaliation as the primary reason. Second was the sense that it was not worth it and the police would do little to assist. Both reasons for not calling the police highlight structural deficiencies that result in impunity. It is a risky proposition to call the police if there is little chance the police are going to catch the perpetrator, and that perpetrator might actually come back when he or she learns that someone called the police.

Overall, the indicators of collective efficacy show that the perceptions of social control have slightly more correspondence with crime in a neighborhood than did observed behavior. Again, that is in line with the collective efficacy hypothesis that perceptions matter more than observed behavior when it comes to social control. The thought that someone would come to the aid of his or her neighbor might mean more than having actually witnessed neighbors aiding one another previously. In any case, there is still no strong indication of correspondence between most indicators and crime.

The indicators of collective efficacy were able to tease out more differences between neighborhoods with more crime and neighborhoods with less crime than the indicators of the social side of disorganization. People in neighborhoods with less crime appear to think about helping one another more than people in neighborhoods with more crime. It appears from these data that policy makers who focus on fixing social order to reduce crime using collective efficacy as a guide are on a little better footing than those on the physical and social side of the disorganization hypothesis.

CORRESPONDENCE BETWEEN CITIZEN SECURITY AND PHYSICAL ORDER

Similar to disorganization and collective efficacy theories, advocates of citizen security policies hypothesize that neighborhoods with physical order should have more responses indicating social order than the neighborhoods with physical disorder. There should be more indications of things like public and private crime-prevention programs and more participation by citizens in those programs in the nicer-looking neighborhoods of Santa Marta and Centro and fewer in rundown neighborhoods of San Ramon and Zacamil. As in the previous analysis, what we would expect to see in Figure 14 are the first two bars for each indicator, representing neighborhoods with physical order, being higher than the second two, representing neighborhoods with physical disorder.

The first indicator, the perception that the municipality adequately supports people's security, shows a great deal of correspondence with physical order. The nicer neighborhoods of Santa Marta and Centro perceived much more work on the part of the municipality than did the rundown neighborhoods of San Ramon and Zacamil. The difference in the second indicator, those who knew of a security program sponsored by the municipality, is also clear. Respondents in nicer neighborhoods knew that their municipality was doing something to prevent crime more than those in rundown areas. Both results support the citizen security hypothesis that municipalities should engage in crime-prevention programs by creating nicer-looking neighborhoods. There is some

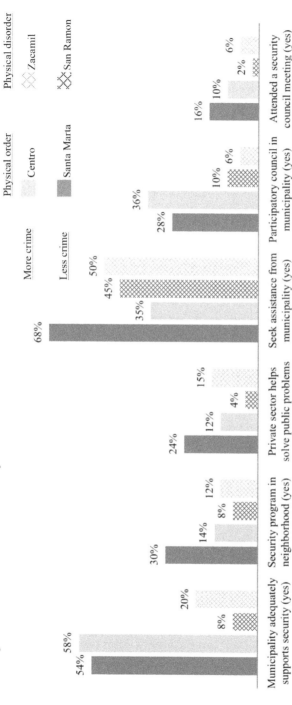

Figure 14. Indicators of Citizen Security

Notes: "Seek assistance" = Municipality as first or second choice from whom to seek assistance among options of family, neighbors, church, municipality, or local organization/association. N=193.

correspondence between the appearance of a neighborhood and the perception of municipal support and action to support security.

These findings are not surprising given the input of interviewees in Santa Tecla praising the role of the municipal preventative police. Preventative police in a number of, but not all, municipalities around San Salvador work to establish a presence in communities beyond that of the national police. While Mejicanos was at only the planning stages for introducing a municipal preventative police force during my fieldwork, Santa Tecla has had an established and visible force for years. Wearing their characteristic white uniforms to distinguish themselves from the blue of the national police, the preventative police in Santa Tecla walk, ride bikes, and station themselves in high-traffic areas. It is likely that this presence added to the sense among respondents that the municipality was engaged in improving security.

Citizen security also hypothesizes that nicer-looking neighborhoods such as Santa Marta and Centro will have more visible involvement by the private sector. There were mixed results on that indicator. Respondents knew of the most involvement by businesses in support of security in Santa Marta. The other nicer-looking neighborhood, Centro, fell below San Ramon, a rundown neighborhood, in involvement by businesses. There is less correspondence than predicted between business support to solve problems and the appearance of a neighborhood.

As seen in the other indicators of social order, there is an important distinction between perceptions and behavior. In citizen security, this is seen most acutely with the number of people who seek assistance from the municipality. Citizen security policy is based on the hypothesis that there is correspondence between how a neighborhood looks and whether people turn to the municipality for help. It predicts that people will turn to the municipality more often in nicer-looking neighborhoods than in rundown neighborhoods. There were mixed results regarding this hypothesis. Respondents in one nicer-looking neighborhood, Santa Marta, did turn to the municipality for help much more often than in any other neighborhood. To the contrary, respondents in the other nicer-looking neighborhood, Centro, turn to the municipality for help less than those in either of the more rundown neighborhoods.

Finally, citizen security is premised on the idea that people in nicer-looking neighborhoods participate more. Instead of general participation in voluntary associations or attending neighborhood events as in disorganization theory, citizen security policy seeks direct participation in the crime-prevention policy process. There is correspondence between the existence of such participatory councils and the physical order of the neighborhoods. Respondents in the nicer-looking neighborhoods knew of more opportunities to participate. The difference was smaller, however, in observed rates of participation. Despite the fact that people in nicer-looking neighborhoods knew of more ways to participate, actual rates of participation were not much higher in nicer-looking neighborhoods than rundown neighborhoods.

Overall, citizen security does a better job of teasing out correspondence between social and physical order than either disorganization or collective efficacy theories. People in nicer-looking neighborhoods perceive action by the municipality to improve security, including through participatory mechanisms, more than people in less-appealing places. Businesses and people in nicer-looking neighborhoods, however, do not appear to participate to increase neighborhood security much differently from people in less-appealing places.

CORRESPONDENCE BETWEEN CITIZEN SECURITY, CRIME, AND VIOLENCE

Citizen security also predicts that we will find a correspondence between indicators of social order and crime and violence. There should be more indications of things like public and private crime-prevention programs and more program participation by citizens in neighborhoods with less crime and violence, and lower participation in neighborhoods with more crime and violence. Looking again at Figure 14, we would expect to see the darker bars for each indicator above their lighter pair. Santa Marta should be higher than Centro (solid bars), and San Ramon should be higher than Zacamil (hatched bars).

Contrary to the theory, the data show that respondents in more-crime neighborhoods actually believe the municipality is supporting their security more than in the less-crime neighborhoods. This is particularly interesting given that knowledge of specific security programs is much higher in the less-crime neighborhood of Santa Marta. Even though respondents in that neighborhood knew of specific municipal programs, they did not believe the municipality was doing enough to prevent crime. Meanwhile, respondents in the other neighborhood with more crime, San Ramon, noted less security support and fewer programs by the municipality than the adjacent neighborhood with more crime, Zacamil. Indeed, there was evidence of greater municipal involvement in crime and violence prevention near Zacamil, where a large recreational facility housed a computer lab, meeting space, and various sporting activities (Figure 15). Meanwhile, there was no clear correspondence between local business support of these types of initiatives and the amount of crime and violence.

The actual behavior of neighbors also shows little correspondence between these indicators and crime and violence. Citizen security approaches assume people will trust and turn to the municipality more often in neighborhoods with less crime and violence than in neighborhoods with more crime and violence. There were mixed results regarding this hypothesis. Respondents in one neighborhood with less crime (Santa Marta) did turn to the municipality for help much more than did those in the bordering neighborhood with more crime (Centro). However, respondents in the other neighborhood with less crime (San Ramon) turn to the municipality for help less than those in the bordering neighborhood with more crime (Zacamil). There is no correspondence between relying on the municipality for assistance and the amount of crime and violence in a neighborhood.

Finally, citizen security policies are based on a hypothesis that people participate directly in the crime-prevention policy process more in neighborhoods with less crime and violence such as Santa Marta and San Ramon. There is no correspondence in

Figure 15. Zacamil– municipal violence- prevention project. (Source: author.)

these data, however, between the knowledge of the existence of such participatory councils or actual participation in the councils and the amount of crime and violence in the neighborhoods. The differences between neighborhoods with more and less crime and violence were small. In both cases at least one neighborhood with more crime and violence had more knowledge of or participation in the councils than its pair with less crime and violence.

Overall, citizen security does a better job of teasing out correspondence between social order and crime and violence than disorganization theory. It does not appear to do any better than collective efficacy theory, however. People in neighborhoods with more crime and violence see the municipality playing an important role in security more than people in neighborhoods with less crime and violence. Similarly, businesses and people in neighborhoods with less crime and violence do not appear to participate to increase neighborhood security much differently from people in neighborhoods with more crime and violence. There is little apparent correspondence overall between the indicators for citizen security and the amount of crime and violence in a neighborhood.

CHAPTER 6

Analyzing the Disorganization Hypothesis

None of the three sets of indicators shows as much difference as expected between the social order of neighborhoods, how much or how little they resemble the kind of place people would say looks "disorderly," or how much crime and violence occurs there. In general, the amount and kinds of social order testified to by the residents in each neighborhood exist independently of what the neighborhoods look like and how much crime and violence occurs there. As we saw in the statistics above, there was only one indicator, how much people trust their neighbors, that fits well with the disorganization hypothesis. People in rundown and crime-ridden neighborhoods trust one another less than people in neighborhoods that look better and have less crime and violence. All the other variables that deal with the way people think about or relate to one another are either unrelated to the neighborhood's physical appearance and crime, or they run counter to what one would expect if the world really worked the way in which proponents of social disorganization theory think it works.

A test of significance applied to these results tells us just how big a difference there is between the disorganization hypothesis and what I found in these neighborhoods. Given that my samples are not random, the test of significance does not help me generalize my findings to a larger universe of places or people. What it does help us see is how large or small the differences we have observed really are. It also helps us know how strongly we can criticize the social disorganization hypothesis in this case.

Table 8 shows the results of a chi-square test of significance applied to the responses by residents of the case study neighborhoods. The procedure tests my findings that there is little or no difference in social order between the neighborhoods in support of the disorganization hypothesis no matter their appearance or the amount of crime that happens in them. Fewer than half of the various ways people have proposed to measure the disorganization hypothesis show any significant difference between the neighborhoods. Those are the indicators with low chi-square values and lack of significance. For these indicators, I cannot reject the "null hypothesis" that there is no difference between the neighborhoods. They are not different enough to suggest any relationship between physical and social order, or social order and crime and violence.

It bears repeating that the only indicator which perfectly fit both parts of the disorganization hypothesis was whether people trust their neighbors. As we see in Table 8, it turns out that the difference between neighborhoods on the trust variable was not significant. In the end, the difference in trust between neighborhoods does not support the disorganization hypothesis as much as predicted. Meanwhile, where there is a significant difference, at least part of those results contradict the disorganization hypothesis as we saw in the discussion in the preceding chapters.

Overall, we have two results from this analysis. The first is a confirmation that there is no big or statistically significant difference between the neighborhoods for a majority of the indicators. The second, in the cases where there is a statistical difference, that difference does not necessarily favor the disorganization hypothesis.

Table 8. Difference in Social Order between Neighborhoods

	x^2
Social Disorganization	
Tight-knit neighborhood	7.52
Trust neighbors	0.72
Neighbors share same values	6.18
Welcome and integrate newcomers	7.94 *
Attend neighborhood events	3.44
Participate in voluntary associations	0.17
Collective Efficacy	
Neighbors get along	2.55
Neighbors willing to help one another	6.80
Neighbors get involved to solve problems	9.90 *
Seek assistance from neighbors	11.21 *
Control exhibited to change impropriety	8.37 *
Police called to report victimization	3.52
Citizen Security	
Municipality adequately supports security	39.35 **
Security program in neighborhood	10.37 *
Private sector helps solve public problems	8.69 *
Seek assistance from municipality	4.34
Participatory council in municipality	17.60 **
Attend a security council meeting	6.76

*$p < .05$, **$p < .01$

In the preceding chapter, I sought to tease out differences in social disorganization using three different, but complementary, sets of indicators. The three sets of indicators came from three hypotheses which all predict that physical order and social order correspond in some way. I did this in an attempt to identify which, if any, set of indicators might be useful for policy makers as they look to remedy crime and violence. I knew from the first part of my analysis that physical order did not correspond to crime and violence. The idea that reformers could prevent crime and violence based on physical interventions alone was already in doubt. I needed to see if fixing the way a place looks had anything to do with fixing how neighbors think about and act around one another. I also needed to see if reformers who decide to intervene directly to fix how people think and act might have a chance of reducing crime and violence.

It was clear in the data that there is little correspondence between the physical and social indicators of disorganization in these neighborhoods. The indicators of social order were not much different between neighborhoods with physical order and neighborhoods with physical disorder. There was more correspondence, however, between collective efficacy and whether a neighborhood was nice or rundown. This correspondence was largely in the perception indicators that are important in collective efficacy. People thought their neighbors got along better and were more willing to help one another in nicer-looking neighborhoods. Finally, citizen security did better than both collective efficacy and disorganization theory in teasing out differences between neighborhoods based on their physical appearance. There was some correspondence between the appearance of a neighborhood and whether a municipality and residents attempt to improve security.

From the literature, I knew that the disorganization hypothesis was on unsure footing. I found that modifications to that hypothesis in collective efficacy and citizen security teased out more correspondence between social and physical order. In the end, however, no matter how we measure social order, there is no strong correspondence between it and physical order in these data. That means that making these neighborhoods look nicer does not necessarily mean that people there will think or act any differently from the way they did before.

In the second look at the data, I wanted to see if there were differences in social order between neighborhoods with more and less crime and violence. I wanted to see if reformers who decide to intervene directly to improve how people think and act had any better chance of reducing crime and violence than those who focus on the physical side. I found that, as expected, the indicators of social order did not correspond well to the amount of crime and violence in a neighborhood. The indicators of collective efficacy and citizen security did a little better, but not much. No matter how I tried to tease out differences, I could not establish correspondence between any set of indicators of social order and crime and violence. This means that doing things like trying to help people get along with their neighbors or participate more in solving their own problems does not necessarily help fix problems like crime and violence.

For policy makers and reformers who propose citizen security interventions in these neighborhoods in El Salvador, it would seem they are on little better footing than proponents of disorganization theory in the United States decades ago. The data show that improvements to a neighborhood's appearance may well improve how the municipality is viewed and increase the number of people who get along. But that increased confidence and civility apparently do not necessarily translate into prevention of crime and violence. Citizen security prescriptions and policy might have rightly gained notoriety for fixing communities, but that success might not actually do anything to prevent crime and violence. Something else is at work that we cannot identify with these indicators.

Before I seek an alternate explanation for the difference in crime and violence between these cases, it bears repeating that these data are not immediately generalizable to other neighborhoods. They are snapshots of four neighborhoods at one moment in time. One could rightly point out that all of these indicators change over time and the cases are not representative of every neighborhood in each municipality, let alone the country. Unfortunately, the breadth and depth of data used here are not available over time and in every neighborhood. Certain data are available, however, that can serve to check my findings against trends in these municipalities and at the national level.

TRENDS AND NATIONAL DATA

To show trends in social disorganization, the data available over time include indicators of security, participation, and cohesion from the Latin American Public Opinion Project. Table 9 summarizes these variables over twenty years for the municipalities in which the neighborhood cases studies were conducted. Participation in the nicer-looking municipality has remained relatively stable over the twenty-year period, even decreasing some from 1999 to 2010. Homicides also decreased from 1999 to 2010. Participation in the more rundown municipality has increased significantly over the same period. Homicides have also increased there. This correspondence in trends suggests that participation actually increases as insecurity increases. It seems that people do get involved to solve problems such as insecurity, but they do so at a greater rate as problems grow more acute. Despite theories to the contrary, there is no evidence here to suggest that participation corresponds to lower rates of crime and violence. It appears the opposite might be true.

Table 9. Trends in Social Disorganization and Crime by Municipality

	Physical order (Santa Tecla)			Physical disorder (Mejicanos)		
	1991	1999	2010	1991	1999	2010
Homicide rate (per 100,000)	-	52.4a	22.1	-	27.7	68.3
Feel very or somewhat safe (agree)	-	66%	51%	-	40%	41%
Participate to solve public problem (yes)	31%	42%	37%	22%	39%	52%
Participate in neighborhood improvement (yes)	13%	17%	14%	24%	14%	32%
Neighbors somewhat or very trustworthy (yes)	39%	67%	63%	29%	50%	83%
N	94	98	49	123	49	44

Notes: ᵃ *Homicide rates 1999–2000. Sources: LAPOP, 2010;* VIML, *2011*

On the other hand, participation seems to correspond better to a sense of security. As respondents in one municipality participated less, they felt less safe despite the fact that violent crime was actually going down in their area. Meanwhile, as respondents in the other municipality participated more, their sense of security remained stable despite a substantial increase in violent crime. Participation there may have helped to mitigate the effects of a spike in violent crime on sense of security. These data picked up on a trend that the snapshot at the neighborhood level was unable to capture. There is evidence to suggest that participation may play some role in improving a sense of security.

The data on trust or cohesion over time were also revealing. The snapshot of the neighborhoods found some difference in level of organization or security no matter the amount of trust or cohesion in a neighborhood. Contrary to the theory that cohesion begets security, trust actually decreased slightly as the homicide rate decreased in one municipality. Further contradicting the theory, trust increased greatly as the homicide rate increased in the other municipality. In terms of sense of security, these data again picked up on something interesting. As trust decreased, so too did sense of security. And as trust increased, the sense of security remained the same despite an increase in crime and violence. The data do not support the hypothesis that increased trust somehow prevents crime and violence. The data do support the hypothesis that trust may play a role in people's sense of security by helping to mitigate the effect of a spike in crime and violence just as participation did.

Interesting as they are, these results are still relevant only to municipalities in which the case study neighborhoods are located. They support some of the findings from the neighborhood-level data and make important distinctions to others. To make sure these cases are not the exception to the rule, the final analysis examines the data available at the national level in El Salvador.

MUNICIPAL VARIATION

The idea that social order varies from municipality to municipality is often taken as a given. I wanted verification that the way people engage with local officials and organize among themselves actually differs between Salvadoran municipalities generally in order to determine if the cases above are in any way representative of other cities. As shown in Table 10 there is indeed a strong association between where someone lives and many indicators of social order. Citizens report differently on the quality of service and engagement with the municipal leaders and police depending on their municipality. They also report on trust and engagement with other members of the community differently depending on where they live.

Associations with indicators of municipal governance hold out for the most part when I examine these same variables against a sense of security. This is especially true of indicators of engagement with police. Police interaction and participation in the community in informal ways are associated with a greater sense of security. Meanwhile, there is much less association between a sense of security and social order. A sense of security is not associated with organizing to solve problems or engaging in community activities. Not surprisingly, indicators that tend to be correlated with a sense of security such as trust and organizing for security show a stronger association. While there is some association between sense of security and social order, there is little or no association between social order and homicide rates. The exception again is with indicators of police engagement and presence that show an association. When we compare these results with those of a sense of security, we see where social order has more to do with perceptions of violence than with actual incidents of violence. However, social order is not a reliable prognosticator of either.

Given these results, there is little difference in social order between more and less secure municipalities. As with the neighborhood cases, I cannot reject the null hypothesis that there is no difference in social order between municipalities with varying levels of a sense of security and homicide rates. The data are not different enough between municipalities to suggest a relationship between social order and crime and violence in El Salvador.

Table 10. Association between Indicators of Social Order, and Crime and Violence

	Municipality	Sense of security	Homicide rate
	x^2	x^2	x^2
Social Order			
Quality of municipal services	181.59**	22.35**	9.74
Attend municipal meeting	96.49**	.30	.44
Request assistance from municipality	60.59	4.40*	1.44
Police converse with residents	110.20**	14.84**	13.61**
Police attend neighborhood meetings	138.28**	2.44	23.35**
Police help in prevention activities	112.87**	22.32**	3.90
Frequency of police patrol in neighborhood	236.60**	34.71**	14.26*
Interpersonal trust	70.37*	81.95**	6.93
Engage to solve problems in the community	78.72**	2.33	1.47
Neighborhood organized for security	63.50	8.28**	3.20
Attend neighborhood association meeting	73.74*	.04	3.24
Attend crime-prevention committee meeting	58.08	2.71	3.47
Attend community-improvement meeting	110.66**	1.28	5.82
Attend political meeting	83.86**	1.53	3.47
Attend religious service	43.56	3.24	4.98
Attend parent meeting	58.32	.10	2.59
Play a team sport	35.35	.04	.73

*$p < .05$, **$p < .01$ Sources: LAPOP, 2014, FUNDAUNGO, 2013

CHAPTER 7

Creating Safe Neighborhoods

Using new and existing data, I examined community and social life in four neighborhoods in detail, and across El Salvador more generally, to try to locate some amount of correspondence between indicators of social and physical order, collective efficacy, citizen security, and crime and violence. That analysis was able to pick up very few of the hypothesized differences. It's not that the data were bad or, as the previous pages demonstrate, that the cases were exceptions to the rule. In these cases, social disorganization theory does not appear to be as predictive of problems such as crime and violence as its proponents would have us believe. This is supported by the fact that the trends and data at the national level also failed to pick up on the predicted differences. While there was some indication at one level or another that participation and cohesion correspond in some way with sense of security, the relationship is far from defined. The data do not tell us if participation and cohesion lead to a sense of security, or if a sense of security leads to participation and cohesion. In any case, the correspondence is with the perception of security, not the actual prevalence of crime and violence such as homicide. Increased participation and trust may make people feel safer, but it does not appear to fix the problem.

The analysis also showed the challenge of determining just how socially ordered or disordered a neighborhood might be. We saw especially where physical order is an imperfect approximation for social order. The physical appearance of a neighborhood does not seem to determine or even reflect the amount of social problems in that neighborhood. This suggests that we cannot simply improve the way a neighborhood looks and expect people to behave better. Based on these findings, we also cannot expect that problems like crime and violence will go away just because neighbors get along better, come together more often, or even exhibit social control.

We now know that a predominant way in which policy makers, planners, and social reformers attempt to prevent crime and violence in El Salvador might not work the way we thought it does. Just because things or people appear out of order does not seem to be the primary way to account for crime and violence in these neighborhoods. However, even creative policy makers need not reinvent the wheel and try to come up with completely new ideas. Plenty of alternatives are offered in the literature and in the experiences of other countries. Once the lens of a particular policy prescription is removed, we are better able to see the whole picture and how social disorganization theory might be improved with lessons from other theories. My methodology allowed me to do just that. I was able to look for patterns in the survey-interview data and to go off-script and explore the stories that interviewees were sharing. A more complete picture emerged with this approach. I explore that picture in the following sections.

BOUNDARIES AND TERRITORY

Most revealing with regard to alternate theories were references that interviewees made not to what happens within their neighborhood but to neighborhood boundaries and the risk involved in crossing those boundaries. The disorganization hypothesis makes little or no reference to the impact of moving across neighborhood boundaries, though we know that boundaries have been crucial to understanding gang conflict and the genesis of interracial violence in U.S. and European cities (Katz, 2008, 2011; Monti, 1994; Pickering, Kintrea, & Bannister, 2012). The disorganization hypothesis looks inward and largely ignores the fact that much of daily life occurs outside of one's own neighborhood. When one must cross through other neighborhoods to go to work or, especially, go to school, local cohesion and efficacy become meaningless and impotent. The amount and variety of social life near one's home matters little once you are outside of the boundaries of your neighborhood. Sometimes even a passing commuter is seen as an unwelcome outsider or, in areas where gang activity is prevalent, an intruder. A sense of security and one's physical safety might therefore be affected just as much by what happens outside of the neighborhood as what happens within it.

This is especially true for children. Take as examples two situations that were offered during interviews. First, a parent whose child just started high school is terrified that her fourteen-year-old must now take the public bus to a different neighborhood to go to school. The child will cross three to four different neighborhoods to get to school. Other high school students will get on the bus along the way. Once the child arrives at the school, classes will be full of students from all different neighborhoods. Given that many primary schools and junior high schools are either in the same building or closer to home, this is the first time many of the children will mix with peers from different neighborhoods. Even if order is maintained within the school, gang members often wait around just outside to recruit new members. Those who resist recruiting efforts can be killed, just as five students in the case study neighborhood of Centro were in the months prior to my interviews (Beltrán Luna, 2012). The parent I interviewed, with little other choice, rides the bus with the fourteen-year old each day and then returns to pick him up for the return trip. Not being there would be agonizing, she says.

As a second example, a public official in charge of recreational activities for children is matter-of-fact about who attends the programs his center offers. The center is located just outside of the case study neighborhood of Zacamil, but still within the municipality of Mejicanos. When asked if any children from Zacamil or San Ramon come to take advantage of the center, the only such center near either neighborhood, he shakes his head. Unfortunately, he told me, children do not come from outside of the immediate area. While they would be welcome at the center and a constant police presence at the center makes it secure, it is too dangerous for them to try to come. He adds that children walking or taking the bus through areas where they are outsiders have been assaulted, or worse.

These are just two anecdotes, but they may be representative of a larger theme. Citizen security may depend less on the social life and organization of adults in a neighborhood than it does on the way they organize the lives of their children. The disorganization hypothesis focuses on all the ways in which adults exercise formal and informal control over values and confront problems in their neighborhoods. It has little to nothing to say about the way those adults organize and move children in and between neighborhoods. These anecdotes and the theme of crossing boundaries take on greater significance when we examine the data on homicide victims' school locations and the literature on territoriality.

In El Salvador, children and adolescents ages 10 to 19 accounted for 26.5 percent of all homicide victims in 2010. The homicide rate for this age group, at 103 per 100,000, is nearly twice the national rate (*IML*, 2010). The disorganization hypothesis fails to offer explanations of why children are more frequently the victims of violence. If physical or social disorder were the only thing at work in a neighborhood, we would expect that people in each age group would have an equal chance of being victimized. That is clearly not the case. School-aged adolescents are more likely to be killed than any other age group. It seems parents and educators are right to be concerned for the well-being of their children.

The concern about children traveling between neighborhoods to go to school also appears valid. Going back to the case study neighborhoods, the more-crime neighborhoods are those where children are coming together from different neighborhoods for the first time to go to public junior high and high schools. The neighborhoods with less crime have no public junior high or high schools where children from different communities come together for the first time (*Ministerio de Educación*, 2011). There are also more private schools in these less-crime neighborhoods. Children attending the public schools are either walking or taking public transportation, while their peers at private schools are being dropped off and picked up at the door in cars. In short, there is more mixing of adolescents in neighborhoods with more crime and less mixing in neighborhoods with less. The literature on territoriality offers perspectives on why this mixing might help explain differences in security between municipalities.

Children and adolescents form a strong sense of territory early on (Pickering, Kintrea, & Bannister, 2012). They know when and, more important, where a group has claimed an area. They know who is an insider in that space and who is an outsider. Both the idea of territoriality and the limitations it places on mobility are well documented from St. Louis (Monti, 1994) to London (Pickering, Kintrea, & Bannister, 2012) and Guatemala City (Winton, 2005). Despite the persistent focus on violence perpetrated by gangs in these places and in San Salvador, violent territorial control is not limited to gangs. Informal neighborhood bands of adolescents and especially school-based groups also exist. This problem has been particularly acute in San Salvador where "hostile" and violent school environments have been a problem since the early twentieth century (Savenije & Beltrán, 2005). No matter who the perpetrators are, the underlying theme is that boundaries and space matter, but potentially not in the way the disorganization hypothesis predicts.

Boundaries guard the identities and interests of those who inhabit a neighborhood. They are an unnatural division between otherwise similar communities. Their existence, as shown in the anecdotes, "reinforce relations—'you–me and us–them'—that structure identities which, in turn, solidify over time" (Katz, 2008, p. 190). Whether a school is across the street or across town, if a boundary is crossed the ingrained "you–me" tension is heightened. As Michael Katz argues (2008, 2011), it is the activation of this tension that determines whether violence will remain under control or become a problem. While the vast majority of children and adolescents do not act on this tension, the few who do limit the mobility of all of the others in public spaces (Winton, 2005).

Just as the disorganization hypothesis posits, those public spaces are important. But maybe not in the way the hypothesis predicts.

Policy prescriptions based on the disorganization hypothesis advocate for well-maintained and orderly public spaces with the hope that these spaces will create greater ownership and cohesion among neighbors. The hypothesis, however, does little to account for the tension between the various groups that claim control over that space. It does even less to deal with the potential for violence when an outside group or individual enters that space. The fact is that public spaces can actually be places that people fear, no matter how ugly or pretty they are. This was the case for many respondents, especially those who live close to *El Paseo* and the park between Centro and Santa Marta. These beautified areas of the neighborhood attracted many people, some from nearby and others from far away. The increased traffic and presence of outsiders overshadowed the attractiveness and opportunities for engagement for many respondents. Instead of making these people feel more secure, the new public spaces actually made them feel less secure.

This points to a paradox in the disorganization hypothesis. It tells us that pretty places make people act better and feel safer. It also tells us that places frequented by outsiders are less cohesive and have more crime. So a pretty place that draws a lot of outsiders, as the public spaces in Centro and Santa Marta do, might make some people feel more secure while others feel less secure. This paradox where public space actually decreases one's sense of security is intensified by the idea of territoriality. Given territorial control of public spaces by certain groups, parks and streets can become places to avoid rather than places for communities to come together (Pickering, Kintrea, & Bannister, 2012; Winton, 2005). Having these public spaces matters. It may be that what neighbors, and especially adolescents, do with them that matters more.

This also leads to a potential critique of the cohesion argument central to the disorganization hypothesis. The anticipated result of policy based on disorganization theory is that neighbors come together through networks and in public spaces to form a tight-knit bond. This focus on what is known as "bonding" or exclusive social capital comes at the expense of "bridging" or inclusive social capital (Putnam, 2000). The disorganization hypothesis ignores the potentially negative effects of strong social cohesion, namely the exclusion of outsiders. In fact, outsiders are seen as a threat by some who focus on physical order (Greenberg, Rohe, & Williams, 1982). They want to design spaces to keep strangers out. The resulting out-group antagonism, increased tension, and potential for increased violence are not taken into account in the disorganization literature or policy prescriptions. In short, there is the potential to do more harm than good by reinforcing boundaries.

Policy makers and planners might therefore need to look beyond neighborhood limits in order to fix problems of crime and violence. As the interviews demonstrate, a child could come from a well-organized, orderly neighborhood, but once she crosses the street into a different neighborhood, that no longer matters. The focus of the disorganization hypothesis on neighborhoods in isolation to determine amounts of crime and problems is insufficient at best, dangerous at worst. Policies and programs based on the theory would be challenged to do much better.

BEYOND NEIGHBORHOODS

If the focus on neighborhoods is insufficient, policy makers and planners may need to remove the lens of neighborhood effects and localized solutions altogether. We may need to look beyond neighborhoods as the sole unit of analysis. It may be that trying to fix crime and violence at the local level is not possible until certain structural problems have been mitigated. A comparison of multiple indicators to determine the amount of crime and violence in a neighborhood reveals a major challenge for interventions at a local level.

We saw that the homicide rate in Santa Tecla declined by more than half in the past ten years while the homicide rate remained the same or even increased around the country. During that period, however, sense of security in Santa Tecla declined by 15 percent (Latin American Public Opinion Project, 2010). Paradoxically, as violence declined, people felt less safe. We saw that the disorganization hypothesis did little to explain this in the case study neighborhoods. What we did not consider were all the various ways in which the larger social and institutional order also affect a sense of security. Even if individuals do not cross boundaries and do not experience the effects of territoriality, structural effects such as impunity and exclusion may still affect their sense of security in their own neighborhoods. It would seem that the disorganization hypothesis does not adequately take the impact of these macro-level problems into consideration.

As illustrated by the interviewee who noted she doesn't bother to call the police anymore given that they do little and doing so puts her at risk, when one cannot presume that the authorities will act, residents fear for their own safety, and the expectation for action from neighbors is diminished. Local policy makers have little to no control over this situation. As good as municipal preventative police might be, even when a perpetrator is caught there is little chance he or she will be convicted of a crime given deficiencies in national institutions. The disorganization hypothesis has not adequately taken into account the role and perceptions of these formal mechanisms of social control, no matter their strength or weakness (Malone, 2010). In social disorganization, the role of the rule of law generally is discounted and replaced by informal mechanisms at the local level (Kubrin & Weitzer, 2003). Encouraging more interaction among neighbors might do little in the face of this impunity, even if it does result in people's getting along better and coming to the aid of one another.

Improving the social organization of a neighborhood also does little to overcome larger structural problems such as exclusion. Even if a neighborhood has strong cohesion and residents feel a tight-knit bond within the local community, that community may still lie at the economic and social margins of society. In fact, poorer areas often exhibit greater levels of cohesion, as residents band together to meet basic needs of food, shelter, community, and security or demand that the state meet their needs (Walton, 2016). Meanwhile, those with more resources can satisfy their needs on their own and do not have to come together as often. The rise in private security that is prevalent in more affluent areas of San Salvador is one example of this personal provision of basic needs on the part of the wealthy. Despite this cohesion in poorer areas, it is most often those areas that suffer most from crime and violence. This points to the potential that the marginalization of whole groups of people, especially youth, may lead to a breakdown in the very idea of coexistence and social contracts that the disorganization hypothesis tries to stitch together. Once they are excluded from the social order that is maintained by a privileged minority, it is not uncommon for youth to reject the society that keeps them at arm's length (Gaborit, 2005; Winton, 2005). Salvadoran gang members in particular point to this marginalization and exclusion as a motivating factor for their delinquency (Lemus & Martínez, 2012).

The macro structures that lead to this marginalization and exclusion in El Salvador include such things as socioeconomic instability, poor social services like basic health care, and a lack of development, education, and employment opportunities (Cruz, 2005). This is not the same as the argument that connects crime and violence to poverty, however. It is not that poverty leads to crime and violence per se, but that the poor are excluded from the opportunities that having money presents. This inequality promotes marginalization and the concentration of disadvantage. The resulting structural barriers either expose individuals to, or protect them from, delinquent behavior, depending on their economic resources (Sampson & Wilson, 1995).

These structural issues have existed in El Salvador for decades and have not been resolved, even through armed conflict (Call, 2002, 2003). New political institutions and economic structures such as neoliberalism may also have exacerbated those tensions to contribute to high levels of violence (Bonner, 2014). No matter the amount of organization we find in neighborhoods, these structures and institutions are difficult, if not impossible, to overcome (Elliot et al., 1996; Kubrin & Weitzer, 2003). We see yet again where the neighborhood as a unit of analysis and the focus of policies and programs might be overly limiting to address the security challenges of the region.

Alternative explanations of crime and violence in Central American cities like Santa Tecla and Mejicanos do not end here. These are only a few of the innumerable ways to approach the problem of crime and violence that came to light during the course of my research. Territoriality, impunity, and exclusion were themes discovered by taking a step back from the disorganization hypothesis to look at the entire picture. These alternate themes demonstrate the fact that it is overly simplistic to attribute crime and violence to a single cause, to examine them in a single unit of analysis, or to treat them through a single level of intervention. They are complex phenomena that require complex policies and programs. Things like cohesion, collective efficacy, and participation at the neighborhood level might be able to help prevent crime and reduce violence only when they occur together with improvements to the rule of law and larger social order. Relying exclusively on any one program theory or another will continue to be insufficient, especially in the complex environment of Central American cities.

Just why the disorganization hypothesis does not appear to hold up in these cases may be related to the particularities of crime and violence in the region. The scope and scale of violence driven by gangs, unfettered by weak states, and consisting of persistent high rates of homicide well in excess of levels ever seen in the United States, combined with low generalized social trust given past armed conflicts, may all overpower the benefits of any amount of social and physical order. These realities point to the overall challenge of international policy transfer (Hare, 2017). In effect, even if social disorganization were proven to relate to crime and violence in Europe or the United States, the very different context in Central America would pose challenges.

This does not mean that neighborhoods should not be studied in the region. In fact, they should be studied more. We need better data at the national and regional levels, but we also must examine the elements of the macro and micro social order that affect a neighborhood. As we have seen, even correspondence in the aggregate between security and trust was not necessarily existent in each neighborhood. We would not have seen this fallacy of division or the complexity of crime and violence without neighborhood-level research. Indeed, policy prescriptions based on the disorganization hypothesis took hold as a result of a lack of this kind of research. We assumed that what worked in one place would work in another, or what did not work in one place might work better somewhere else. We were afraid of reinventing the wheel, so proper due diligence to see if the wheel needed adjustments might have been overlooked.

We should also not discard further dialogue about improving the citizen security approach in El Salvador and Central America. Citizen security policies are continually proposed and adopted in municipalities and legislatures in the region. In fact, Mayor Óscar Ortiz of Santa Tecla became vice president based in part on his success in promoting citizen security at the municipal level. His tenure as mayor saw the creation of a preventative police force, creation of *El Paseo*, rehabilitation of parks, creation of participatory crime-prevention councils, and other citizen security approaches. However, his public discourse now as vice president favors a more repressive approach. This may reflect the challenges of implementing citizen security approaches at the national level, or it may suggest the need to complement citizen security approaches at the local level with increased police and military force such as the soldiers I saw along *El Paseo*. In any case, it demonstrates that citizen security is not a closed conversation by any means in El Salvador or the region.

The goal of this research at the outset was not to debunk the disorganization hypothesis or a specific policy or program. In fact, after visiting *El Paseo*, reading about citizen security interventions, and discussing policies and programs with local officials, I was a believer. With the results presented here, however, I now recognize even more that we must carefully examine the theories that undergird all policies and programs no matter who is prescribing them. In the end, policy makers and planners in Salvadoran neighborhoods will never be completely freed from the prescriptions of international agencies. They need the financial resources tied to those prescriptions, and they lack the time and human resources to fully evaluate all options. Using what resources they can muster, they must advocate for evidence-based interventions.

In the cases presented here, I found little evidence to support interventions based on the disorganization hypothesis in these neighborhoods. However, the myth that *zonas peligrosas* are less socially and physically ordered neighborhoods has taken hold through sheer force of repetition. It plays on the real desire to improve communities and show tangible changes to confront the intractable problem of crime and violence in neighborhoods. In the cases presented here, increased order may indeed improve the community life of these neighborhoods in some way, but it appears to do little to prevent crime and violence.

Bibliography

Abt, T., & Wiship, C. (2016). *What works in reducing community violence: A meta-review and field study for the Northern Triangle.* Bethesda, MD: Democracy International.

Alcaldía Municipal de Santa Tecla (2012). *Plan estratégico participativo 2012-2022* [Participatory strategic plan 2012-2022]. Unpublished government document.

Beltrán Luna, J. (2012, July 20). *Maras masacraron a cinco estudiantes* [Gangs kill five students]. *El Diario de Hoy.* Retrieved from http://www.elsalvador.com.

Bergman, M. (2006). Crime and citizen security in Latin America: The challenges for new scholarship. *Latin American Research Review, 41*(2), 213-227.

Bonner, M. (2014). Violence, policing and citizen (in)security. *Latin American Research Review, 49*(1), 261-269.

Call, C. (2002). War transitions and the new civilian security in Latin America. *Comparative Politics, 35*(1), 1-20.

Call, C. (2003). War and state-building: Constructing the rule of law in El Salvador. *Journal of Latin American Studies, 35*(4), 827-862.

Chinchilla, L. (2003). Citizen participation in crime prevention. In H. Frühling & J. Tulchin, *Crime and violence in Latin America:*

Citizen security, democracy and the state (pp. 205–232). Washington, DC: Woodrow Wilson Center Press.

Cruz, J. M. (2005). Los factores asociados a las pandillas juveniles en Centroamérica [Factors associated with gangs in Central America]. Estudios Centroamericanos, 60(685–686), 1155–1182.

Cruz, J. M., & Santacruz Giralt, M. (2005, April). La victimización y la percepción de seguridad en El Salvador en 2004 [Victimization and the perception of security in El Salvador in 2004]. San Salvador: UCA Editores. Retrieved from http://www.uca.edu.sv.

Dirección General de Estadísticas y Censos (2007). VI Censo de población y V de vivienda 2007 [VI Population and V housing census 2007]. Retrieved from http://www.digestyc.gob.sv.

Elliot, D., Wilson, W., Huizinga, D., Sampson, R., Elliot, A., & Rankin, B. (1996). The effects of neighborhood disadvantage on adolescent development. Journal of Research in Crime and Deliquency, 34(4), 389–426.

Escobar, G. (2012). Using social disorganization theory to understand the spatial distribution of homicides in Bogotà, Colombia. Revista INVI, 74(27), 21–85.

Esri. (2014). Esri maps and apps. Retrieved from http://esri.maps.arcgis.com.

Frühling, H. (2012). La eficacia de las políticas públicas de seguridad ciudadana en América Latina y el Caribe [The effectiveness of citizen security policy in Latin America and the Caribbean]. Washington, DC: Inter-American Development Bank. Retrieved from http://www.iadb.org.

Frühling, H., & Gallardo, R. (2012). Programas de seguridad dirigidos a barrios en la experiencia chilena reciente [Security programs aimed at neighborhoods, the recent Chilean experience]. Revista INVI, 75(27), 149–185.

FUNDAUNGO (2013). Atlas de la violencia en El Salvador [Atlas of violence in El Salvador]. San Salvador: Talleres Gráficos UCA.

Gaborit, M. (2005). Los círculos de la violencia: violencia social y procesos comunitarios [Circles of violence: Social violence and community processes]. Pensamiento Psicológico, 1(5), 107–116.

Gans, H. (1962). The urban villagers: Group and class in the life of Italian-Americans. New York: The Free Press.

Greenberg, S., Rohe, W., & Williams, J. (1982). Safety in urban neighborhoods: A comparison of physical characteristics and informal territorial control in high and low crime neighborhoods. Population and Environment, 5(3), 141–165.

Guerrero Velasco, R., Gutiérrez Martínez, M. I., Fandiño-Losada, A., & Cardona, S. (2012). *Sistema de indicadores comparables de convivencia y seguridad ciudadana: Un consenso de países* [System of comparable indicators of coexistence and citizen security: A consensus among countries]. *Revista Panamericana de Salud Pública, 31*(3), 253–259.

Guerry, A. (1833). *Essai sur la statistique morale de la France* [Moral statistics of France]. Paris: Crochard.

Hall, P. (2002). *Cities of tomorrow: An intellectual history of urban planning and design in the twentieth century.* Hoboken, NJ: Wiley-Blackwell.

Hare, T. (2017). Policy transfer in international development: Whose security in Central America? *Reconsidering Development, 5*(1).

Instituto de Medicina Legal. (2011). *Epidemiología de los homicidios en El Salvador año 2010.* San Salvador: *Corte Suprema de Justicia.*

Jacobs, J. (1961). *The death and life of great American cities.* New York: Random House.

Katz, M. (2008). Why don't American cities burn very often? *Journal of Urban History, 34*(2), 185–208.

Katz, M. (2011). *Why don't American cities burn?* Philadelphia: University of Pennslyvania Press.

Kelling, G., & Wilson, J. (1982, March). Broken windows: The police and neighborhood safety. *The Atlantic.* Retrieved from http://www.theatlantic.com.

Klein, M. (1995). *The American street gang: Its nature, prevalence, and control.* New York: Oxford University Press.

Kubrin, C., & Weitzer, R. (2003). New directions in social disorganization theory. *Journal of Research in Crime and Deliquency, 40*(4), 374–402.

Labrador Aragón, G., & Sanz, J. (2012, February 22). *La impunidad en los homicidios alcanza el 96%, según ministro de seguridad* [Impunity reaches 96%, according to security minister]. *El Faro.* Retrieved from http://www.elfaro.net.

Latin American Public Opinion Project. (2010). *AmericasBarometer.* Nashville: Vanderbilt University. Retrieved from http://www.vanderbilt.edu/lapop.

Latin American Public Opinion Project. (2014). *AmericasBarometer.* Nashville: Vanderbilt University. Retrieved from http://www.vanderbilt.edu/lapop.

Lees, A. (1991). *Cities perceived: Urban society in European and American thought, 1820–1940*. Manchester: Manchester University Press.

Lemus, E., & Martínez, C. (2012, March 19). *Raúl Mijango hace público comunicado conjunto de la Mara Salvatrucha y el Barrio 18* [Raúl Mijango publicizes joint press release by Mara Salvatrucha and Barrio 18 gangs]. *El Faro*. Retrieved from www.elfaro.net.

Malone, M. (2010). The verdict is in: The impact of crime on public trust in Central American justice systems. *Journal of Politics in Latin America, 2*(3), 99–128.

Meléndez, C. (2014, March 16). *FMLN en multitudinaria celebración electoral* [Mass electoral celebration for FMLN]. *La Prensa Gráfica*, 12.

Ministerio de Educación, República de El Salvador. (2011). *Base oficial de centros escolares 2011* [Official school database 2011]. Retrieved from http://mined.gob.sv.

Monti, D. (1994). *Wannabe.* New York: Wiley.

Newman, O. (1972). *Defensible space: Crime prevention through urban design.* New York: Macmillan.

Observatorio Municipal para la Prevención de la Violencia. (2012). *Comportamiento de las incidencias delictivas* [Incidents of criminal behavior]. Unpublished government document.

Olavarría-Gambi, M., & Allende-González, C. (2014). Crime in neighborhoods: Evidence from Santiago, Chile. *Crime Prevention and Community Safety, 16*(3), 205–226.

Park, R. E. (1915). The city: Suggestions for the investigation of human behavior in the city environment. *American Journal of Sociology, 20*, 577–612.

Park, R. E., & Burgess, E. W. (1925). *The city: Suggestions for investigation of human behavior in the urban environment.* Chicago: University of Chicago Press.

Pickering, J., Kintrea, K., & Bannister, J. (2012). Invisible walls and visible youth: Territoriality among young people in British cities. *Urban Studies, 49*(5), 945–960.

Putnam, R. (2000). *Bowling alone: The collapse and revival of American community.* New York: Simon & Schuster.

Rawson, R. (1839). An inquiry into the statistics of crime in England and Wales. *Journal of the Statistical Society of London, 2*, 316–344.

Sampson, R. (2004). Neighbourhood and community: Collective efficacy and community safety. *New Economy, 11*(2), 106–113.

Sampson, R. (2009). Disparity and diversity in the contemporary city: Social (dis)order revisited. *The British Journal of Sociology, 60*(1), 1–31.

Sampson, R. (2012). *Great American city: Chicago and the enduring neighborhood effect.* Chicago: University of Chicago Press.

Sampson, R., & Groves, W. B. (1989). Community structure and crime: Testing social-disorganization theory. *The American Journal of Sociology, 94*(4), 774–802.

Sampson, R., & Raudenbush, S. (1999). Systematic social observation of public spaces: A new look at disorder in urban neighborhoods. *American Journal of Sociology, 105*(3), 603–651.

Sampson, R., Raudenbush, S., & Earls, F. (1997). Neighborhoods and violent crime: A multilevel study of collective efficacy. *Science, 277*(5328), 918–924.

Sampson, R., & Wilson, W. (1995). Toward a theory of race, crime, and urban inequality. In J. Hagan & R. Peterson (eds.), *Crime and inequality.* Stanford: Stanford University Press.

Savenije, W., & Beltrán, M. (2005). *Compitiendo en bravuras: Violencia estudiantil en el área metropolitana de San Salvador* [Competing ferocity: Student violence in the San Salvador metropolitan area]. San Salvador: *Facultad Latinoamericana de Ciencias Sociales.* Retrieved from http://www.flacso.org.sv.

Segura, E. (2013, March 6). *Inseguridad, principal reclamo ciudadano* [Insecurity, primary concern of citizens]. *La Prensa Gráfica,* 22–23.

Segura, E. (2014, January 17). *La delincuencia es lo que más preocupa* [Delinquency is top concern]. *La Prensa Gráfica.* Retrieved from www.laprensagrafica.com.

Shaw, C. (1929). *Deliquency areas: A study of the geographic distribution of school truants, juvenile delinquents, and adult offenders in Chicago.* Chicago: University of Chicago Press.

Shaw, C., & McKay, H. (1942). *Juvenile deliquency and urban areas.* Chicago: University of Chicago Press.

Silva, B. (2014). Social disorganization and crime: Searching for the determinants of crime at the community level. *Latin American Research Review, 49*(3), 219–230.

Sosa, B. (2012, August 30). *Espacio público para prevención social* [Public space for social prevention]. *La Prensa Gráfica,* 20.

Spergel, I. (1995). *The youth gang problem: A community approach.* New York: Oxford University Press.

Suttles, G. (1968). *The social order of the slum.* Chicago: University of Chicago Press.

Timerman, J. (2013, October 1). Why international aid agencies are starting to focus on urban violence. *The Atlantic.* Retrieved from http://www.theatlanticcities.com/.

Tulchin, J., & Golding, H. (2003). Citizen security in regional perspective. In H. Frühling & J. Tulchin, *Crime and violence in Latin America: Citizen security, democracy and the state* (pp. 205–232). Washington, DC: Woodrow Wilson Center Press.

United Nations Development Programme (2005). *Informe sobre desarrollo humano: El Salvador 2005* [Human development report: El Salvador 2005]. San Salvador: UNDP.

United Nations Development Programme (2009a). *Academic programme in citizen security: A tool for influencing public policy.* Washington, DC: UNDP.

United Nations Development Programme (2009b). *Community security and social cohesion: Towards a UNDP approach.* New York: UNDP.

United Nations Development Programme (2009c). *Opening spaces to citizen security and human development: Human development report for Central America.* New York: UNDP.

United Nations Development Programme (2009d). *Almanaque 262: Estudio de desarollo humano en los municipios de El Salvador 2009* [Almanac 262: Study of human development in Salvadoran municipalities 2009]. San Salvador: UNDP.

United Nations Development Programme (2013). *Citizen security with a human face: Evidence and proposals for Latin America.* New York: UNDP.

United Nations Office on Drugs and Crime (2007). *Crime and development in Central America: Caught in the crossfire.* Vienna: UNODC.

United States Agency for International Development (2010). *Como trabajar, de forma participativa, en la prevención de la violencia y la delincuencia a nivel local* [How to work, via participation, in the prevention of violence and deliquency at the local level]. San Salvador: USAID.

Valenzuela Aguilera, A. (2012). Collective efficacy as a social control strategy of space: Evidence from Cuernavaca, Mexico. *Revista INVI*, *74*(27), 187-215.

Villareal, A., & Silva, B. (2006). Social cohesion, criminal victimization and perceived risk of crime in Brazilian neighborhoods. *Social Forces*, *84*(3), 1725-1753.

Walton, E. (2016). "It's not just a bunch of buildings": Social psychological investment, sense of community, and collective efficacy in a multiethnic low-income neighborhood. *City & Community*, *15*(3), 231-263.

Washington Office on Latin America & Inter-American Development Bank. (2011). *MAPEO de las intervenciones de seguridad ciudadana en Centroamérica financiadas por la cooperación internacional* [Mapping of citizen security initiatives in Central America financed by international agencies]. Retrieved from http://www.wola.org.

Wells, M. (2013, December 11). El Salvador mass graves put pressure on gang truce. *InSight Crime: Organized Crime in the Americas*. Retrieved from http://www.insightcrime.org.

Whyte, W. F. (1943). *Street corner society: The social structure of an Italian slum*. Chicago: University of Chicago Press.

Winton, A. (2005). Youth, gangs and violence: Analysing the social and spatial mobility of young people in Guatemala City. *Children's Geographies*, *3*(2), 167-184.

Wirth, L. (1938). Urbanism as a way of life. *American Journal of Sociology*, *44*, 1-24.

World Bank, The (2011). *World development report 2011: Conflict, security and development*. Washington, DC: The World Bank Group.

Reviews of Tom Hare's monograph
ZONAS PELIGROSAS: THE CHALLENGE OF CREATING SAFE NEIGHBORHOODS IN CENTRAL AMERICA
DANIEL J. MONTI

Three persons reviewed the Hare manuscript:

Hugo Frühling, Director
Instituto de Asuntos Públicos
Universidad de Chile

Mauricio Gaborit
Jefe, Departamento de Psicología
Director, Maestría Intervención Social
Universidad Centroamericana "José Simeón Cañas"
San Salvador, El Salvador

Dr. Mary Frances Malone
Department of Political Science
University of New Hampshire

All three liked the manuscript. That alone wouldn't have guaranteed the monograph's acceptance to the *Polis* series any more than one or even two mediocre reviews or one negative review would have sunk its chances. It all depends on how reasonably the reviewers addressed the author's argument and whether they could offer good suggestions as to what the author might do to improve it. Equally important, the author needed to engage with the external reviewers and be willing to make revisions to improve the manuscript or provide arguments as to why a change wouldn't support his theory.

The author addressed all three reviewers' comments and suggestions in the final manuscript.

I ask prospective authors for the names of persons they think might like the manuscript or might not like the manuscript. I invite both to comment on a submission. In this case, only Mauricio Gaborit was familiar with Hare's work. He lives near the suburbs Hare studied and consulted often with him. I figured he would like the manuscript.

For his part, Hare was familiar with Hugo Frühling's work and spoke of it approvingly. He didn't know Professor Malone or her work. I found Malone in a Google search, checked out her work, and pitched her Hare's topic. Both Frühling and Malone were gracious enough to review the manuscript. Neither Hare nor I had a guess as to how positively they would review it. All we knew was that both were well qualified to comment on its content.

Predictably, Gaborit was more effusive in his comments:

> The study squarely addresses the quandary of major stakeholders that have to decide between policies where prevention measures compete for limited resources and a place in social imagination and repressive measures. It is not an easy decision, and the study provides both theoretical and empirical evidence that may help those responsible for policy formulation and implementation to sort out the dangers of a one-sided preference. This is especially pertinent because politicians are very keen to public sentiment and, for quite some time in El Salvador, the public sentiment leans toward "*mano dura*" (repressive measures). The subject matter and its treatment in the research

reported are very timely and can contribute to new policy for-mulation on a topic that still defines major political discussions in El Salvador. This is particularly true because the discourse of the then-candidate and now vice president of El Salvador has metamorphosed toward repressive measures. A more nuanced approach as is evidenced in the study reported is much needed.

Frühling did a fine job suggesting holes that Hare needed to fill:

There are some questions regarding theory. The first is that some Latin American authors have done a few studies with empirical data based on the ecology of crime theory, and I think it would be interesting if the author reviewed them. I could sug-gest a few of them if you are interested.

There are differences among proponents of the theory and it would be unfair to put them in the same bag. Sampson is critical of broken windows. Bursik advances the idea of public control, which the author could analyze with his own data. For instance, do neighborhoods that attract more attention from the state have less crime? Finally, I think citizen security is not a theory, although the banner describes a certain understanding of what works and what does not.

Maybe more should be said about the methodology. How were the neighborhoods selected? Are these four disadvantaged neighborhoods with similar social indicators? How big they are or populous? Are there external factors that might explain more crime in some of them (presence of criminal gangs per-haps, fewer policemen)?

The final analysis may require clarification. I totally agree that intervention focused on individual neighborhoods might not reduce overall crime. However, I am not very clear as to what the author suggests as an alternative. When it comes to focusing on children, Sampson himself suggested that was one manifestation of collective efficacy.

Malone, too, was complimentary but saw ways in which Hare could improve his manuscript:

I'd like to learn a lot more about how residents use public spac-es in each of the four cases, how do they come together if there are no safe places, and how they participate in decision-making processes. One of the benefits of qualitative case studies is that we can incorporate rich narrative and qualitative detail. The author does not really take advantage of this benefit of the research design. We get a superficial overview of each case, so that the author can classify it as low/high social order and low/high physical disorder.

The author notes in passing that the United States and many European countries have faced similar challenges in terms of physical and social disorder earlier in their histories. I think this is an interesting way to frame this study, and I think it would be great to learn more about these similarities and place contemporary El Salvador into a broader historical and theoretical context.

One glaring omission is that the nature of the crime crisis in El Salvador is quite different from that of most other countries where such theories have been developed—the crime epidemic is driven by organized criminal groups, *maras*, who have systematically challenged the state's monopoly of force. Furthermore, homicide rates in El Salvador have consistently ranked among the highest in the world. Indeed, in Table 4, even the low homicide rate municipalities report rates four and five times higher than the U.S. average, and more than double the rate that international organizations consider to be detrimental to a country's governance and economy. Given very different scope and scale of *mara*-related crime, there is strong reason to suspect that social disorganization theories will do a poor job of explaining patterns in contemporary El Salvador. The author should discuss this in greater depth and be more creative when applying these theories to a very different national context.

I think it is good to note that the empirical evidence from these four communities questions the theoretical underpinnings of contemporary citizen security policies. But the author needs to stop there, as the results are not generalizable and there is no alternative story to tell.

It's hard to get thoughtful reviews that point out spots where an article could be improved while avoiding criticism of the author for the paper the reviewers think he should have written. Both the Frühling and Malone reviews hit the mark on both counts. In his response to the reviewers, Hare said he would revise his manuscript so that it would address all of their concerns. That, too, is something that editors and editorial boards look for.

Had Hare taken exception to any of their suggestions, he would have been well within his rights to defend his work. Fred Nachbaur, Fordham University Press's director, and I, the editor for the *Polis* series, would have then discussed the pros and cons of the exchange and determine what step(s) to take next. In this case, that wasn't necessary. Hare amended his essay according to ideas the reviewers suggested, and we gave final approval to the manuscript.

I was drawn to the manuscript for all the reasons noted by the outside reviewers. There is no idea more central to the study of urban life than "social disorganization." I would have liked Hare to give an even more thorough treatment of the intellectual origins of this concept. However, I think he did a commendable job and made a genuine contribution by pointing out how the idea had traveled and been applied in a different location and context. His analysis of the crime and social capital data was clear. His appreciation for the limits of what he could say and do with these data was evident. Both academic researchers and policy wonks would be well advised not to take even our most cherished theories uncritically. Hare did us all a service by holding this particularly important idea up to the light and showing us how well it worked out in practice. It's a fine essay.

Lightning Source UK Ltd.
Milton Keynes UK
UKHW04f1256070918
328484UK00001B/69/P